HUMANISM

Second edition

Definitions of humanism as educational movement, philosophical concept or existential 'life stance' have evolved over the centuries as the term has been adopted for a variety of cultural and political purposes and contexts. Reactions against humanism have contributed to movements such as structuralism, postmodernism and postcolonialism.

Tony Davies offers a clear introduction to the many uses of this influential yet complex concept, and this second edition extends his discussion to include:

- *a wide-ranging history of the development of the term and its influences*
- *the implications of debates around humanism and post-humanism for political, religious and environmental activists*
- *discussion of the key figures in humanist debate from Erasmus and Milton to Heidegger, Foucault and Chomsky*
- *a new glossary and further reading section.*

Offering clear explanations and pertinent discussions, this volume is essential reading for anyone approaching the study of humanism, post-humanism or critical theory.

Tony Davies was formerly Professor and Head of the English Department at the University of Birmingham, from which he recently retired. He has edited Milton's poetry and prose, and written on renaissance and modern literature, literary theory and the teaching of English.

THE NEW CRITICAL IDIOM

SERIES EDITOR: JOHN DRAKAKIS, UNIVERSITY OF STIRLING

The New Critical Idiom is an invaluable series of introductory guides to today's critical terminology. Each book:

- provides a handy, explanatory guide to the use (and abuse) of the term
- offers an original and distinctive overview by a leading literary and cultural critic
- relates the term to the larger field of cultural representation

With a strong emphasis on clarity, lively debate and the widest possible breadth of examples, *The New Critical Idiom* is an indispensable approach to key topics in literary studies.

Also available in this series:

HUMANISM

Second edition

Tony Davies

Routledge
Taylor & Francis Group

LONDON AND NEW YORK

First edition published 1997
by Routledge
Second edition published 2008
by Routledge
2 Park Square, Milton Park, Abingdon OX14 4RN

Simultaneously published in the USA and Canada
by Routledge
270 Madison Ave, New York, NY 10016

Reprinted 2008 (twice)

Routledge is an imprint of the Taylor & Francis Group, an informa business

© 1997, 2008 Tony Davies

Typeset in Garamond and Scala Sans by
Taylor & Francis Books
Printed and bound in Great Britain by
TJ International Ltd, Padstow, Cornwall

British Library Cataloguing in Publication Data
A catalogue record for this book is available from the British Library

Library of Congress Cataloging in Publication Data
Davies, Tony, 1940-
Humanism / Tony Davies. – 2nd ed.
p. cm.
Includes bibliographical references and index.
　1. Humanism. I. Title.
　　B105.H8D38 2008
　　144–dc22

　　　　　　　　2007028808

ISBN 10: 0-415-42064-4 (hbk)
ISBN 10: 0-415-42065-2 (pbk)
ISBN 10: 0-203-93256-0 (ebk)

ISBN 13: 978-0-415-42064-8 (hbk)
ISBN 13: 978-0-415-42065-5 (pbk)
ISBN 13: 978-0-203-93256-8 (ebk)

CONTENTS

SERIES EDITOR'S PREFACE

The New Critical Idiom is a series of introductory books which seeks to extend the lexicon of literary terms, in order to address the radical changes which have taken place in the study of literature during the last decades of the twentieth century. The aim is to provide clear, well-illustrated accounts of the full range of terminology currently in use, and to evolve histories of its changing usage.

The current state of the discipline of literary studies is one where there is considerable debate concerning basic questions of terminology. This involves, among other things, the boundaries which distinguish the literary from the non-literary; the position of literature within the larger sphere of culture; the relationship between literatures of different cultures; and questions concerning the relation of literary to other cultural forms within the context of interdisciplinary studies.

It is clear that the field of literary criticism and theory is a dynamic and heterogeneous one. The present need is for individual volumes on terms which combine clarity of exposition with an adventurousness of perspective and a breadth of application. Each volume will contain as part of its apparatus some indication of the direction in which the definition of particular terms is likely to move, as well as expanding the disciplinary boundaries within which some of these terms have been traditionally contained. This will involve some re-situation of terms within the larger field of cultural representation, and will introduce examples from the area of film and the modern media in addition to examples from a variety of literary texts.

INTRODUCTION
WHAT IS HUMANISM?

Well, that depends, as the boring old adage goes, on what you *mean* by 'humanism'. The first question, as always, is the question of definition. So let's start with a dictionary – or rather, with the daughter of a famous dictionary-maker.

> 'There's glory for you!'
>
> 'I don't know what you mean by "glory",' Alice said.
>
> Humpty Dumpty smiled contemptuously. 'Of course you don't – till I tell you. I meant, "there's a nice knock-down argument for you!"'
>
> 'But "glory" doesn't mean "a nice knock-down argument",' Alice objected.
>
> 'When I use a word,' Humpty Dumpty said, in a rather scornful tone, 'it means just what I choose it to mean – neither more nor less.'
>
> (Carroll 1965: 268–69)

The Alice for whom Charles Lutwidge Dodgson, writing as 'Lewis Carroll', invented her namesake's fantastic adventures through the looking-glass was Alice Liddell, the seven-year-old daughter of Henry George Liddell, ex-headmaster of Westminster School, Dean of Christ Church, Oxford, and compiler, with his colleague Robert Scott, of a monumentally authoritative *Greek–English Lexicon* whose 1800 pages encompassed the full variety – historical, etymological, geographical, grammatical, morphological – of ancient Greek, illustrated by examples drawn from virtually every extant author from the tragedian Achaeus Eritreius to the historian Zosimus. First published in 1843, and known to generations of scholars and students simply as 'Liddell and Scott', the *Lexicon* borrowed its descriptive methodology and much of its material from the philological researches of Franz Passow, Professor of Greek at the University of Breslau, and Georg Curtius, his contemporary at Prague and Leipzig; for while the language and literature of the ancient Greeks continued to be studied in British schools and universities, as it had been since the sixteenth century, the truly pioneering work on Greek and its sister Indo-European languages was being done, in the nineteenth century, in Germany.

The motivation behind the great resurgence of German philological and historical scholarship was a reformed educational system inspired by the romantic Hellenism of Winckelmann and Goethe; and the word the reformers coined to describe their educational ideals, with a backward glance to the classical *studia humanitatis* or 'study of humanity' promoted by the *umanisti* or educators of an earlier 'renaissance', was *Humanismus*: humanism.

Humanism is a word with a very complex history and an unusually wide range of possible meanings and contexts; and for anyone attempting to offer an account of those meanings, the attraction of Humpty Dumpty's approach to the problems of definition is obvious. Life would certainly be much easier, and this book a good deal more straightforward, if I could simply set out my definition of humanism on the first page, and then proceed to demonstrate, with carefully selected examples and a contemptuous disregard for any prosaic objections, that it means just what I choose it to mean.

No such luck, however. The seven distinct sub-definitions of humanism rather conservatively offered by the *Oxford English*

Dictionary represent only a fraction of the senses and contexts in which the word has been used, and a drastic simplification of those. It is one of those words, like 'realism' or 'romanticism', whose range of possible uses runs from the pedantically narrow to the cosmically vague. Like them, too, it carries, even in the most neutrally descriptive contexts, powerful connotations, both positive and negative, of ideological allegiance, its very imprecision making it all the more serviceable as a shibboleth of approval or condemnation. To some modern humanists, the contributors to Julian Huxley's *The Humanist Frame* (1961), for example, it stands self-evidently for the secular and rational decencies of contemporary 'western' civilisation (i.e. of people like themselves); while at the other extreme, I have seen two normally quite civilised and peaceable academics almost come to blows after one accused the other's latest book of 'residual humanism', a description which was taken, and intended, as an insult of the most offensive kind. On this subject at least, one person's 'glory' really can mean another's 'nice knock-down argument'.

Although Humpty Dumpty himself, unlike some of his colleagues in the Alice stories, is not strictly speaking an allegorical figure, he is certainly more than a piece of harmless drollery borrowed from a well-known children's rhyme. The mathematician Dodgson, as a young Fellow of Liddell's Christ Church in the 1850s and 1860s, was at the epicentre of the theological ructions caused by the Catholic-inspired Oxford Movement and the row precipitated by the publication of the doctrinally heretical *Essays and Reviews* (1860). Both of these, in their contrasting ways, were reactions to another kind of 'humanism': a secular rationalism and scientific positivism that drew sustenance from the work of scientists like the geologist Charles Lyell and his friend Charles Darwin, work that seemed to many to be undermining the foundations of Christianity. Humpty has been described as 'Verbal Inspiration sitting on a wall of scripture' (Taylor 1952: 123), High Church orthodoxy entrenched in an authoritarian biblical theodicy ('there's glory for you'), and his fall has been associated with the dismay occasioned in the Anglican faithful, among whom the Reverend Dodgson would have numbered himself, when two of the contributors to the knock-down arguments of *Essays and Reviews*, who had been arraigned for heresy before an ecclesiastical court, were acquitted on appeal by the King's men of the Privy Council (Crowther 1970: 20–35).

But Humpty is also a philologist, a linguistic no less than a theological authority; and humanism, as we shall see, is inseparable from the question of language. 'Man', in the old definition (often attributed to Aristotle), is the 'talking animal'. The fifteenth-century Florentine *umanisti* from whom the word ultimately derives were above all language teachers, rhetoricians, translators, and the tools they forged for their trade were the lexicon and the glossary. According to Samuel Johnson's *Dictionary*, with its sardonic definition of a lexicographer ('a writer of dictionaries; a harmless drudge that busies himself in tracing the original, and detailing the signification of words'), a humanist is 'a grammarian; a philologer', a definition that suggests how low those noble occupations had fallen by the later eighteenth century. Even Humpty, in whose withering presence words surrender their autonomy and meekly submit to the meanings he prescribes for them, could justify his linguistic terrorism with a kind of etymological authority. For Alice is wrong: 'glory' really can mean 'a nice knock-down argument'. One of the oldest meanings of the word is 'exulting over the defeat of an enemy', as the contributors to *Essays and Reviews* exulted, or gloried, in the humiliating 'knock-down' of their clerical persecutors. In short, he is, like Alice's father, a lexicographer.

When Dodgson wrote, 'humanism' was a word of recent coinage; but already the complex of ideas to which it referred was associated with (another nineteenth-century word) the 'Renaissance', a dauntingly complicated constellation of political, cultural and intellectual developments in fifteenth-century Europe whose very existence is dismissed by some twentieth-century historians as a fiction, even while others continue to identify it as the intellectual cradle of the modern world (Burke 1987: 5) The resulting accumulation and contest of meanings is densely impacted and at times explosively controversial. On one side, humanism is saluted as the philosophical champion of human freedom and dignity, standing alone and outnumbered against the battalions of ignorance, tyranny and superstition. For Matthew Arnold, whose work has exerted incalculable influence in shaping educational thinking in the English-speaking world, it is synonymous with the 'culture' to which we must look as the only bulwark against the materialistic 'anarchy' of contemporary society (Arnold 1869). On the other, it has been denounced as an ideological smokescreen for the oppressive mystifications of modern society and culture, the marginalisation and oppression of the multitudes of human beings in whose name it pretends to speak, and even, through an inexorable 'dialectic of enlightenment', for the nightmare of fascism and the atrocity of total war (Adorno 1973: 51, 107). In one sense or another it has helped to articulate all the major themes of the continuously unfolding revolution of modernity, structuring key concepts and debates in politics, science, aesthetics, philosophy, religion and education; and in spite of the anachronistic crankiness of some contemporary 'humanist' movements, and the damage inflicted by a variety of philosophical antihumanisms (some of which will be explored in later chapters), the question of humanism remains ideologically and conceptually central to modern – perhaps even to 'postmodern' – concerns.

This is the tangle that I shall try to unravel in the pages that follow: not in the hope of rescuing a single stable 'meaning', or even a range of sharply focused definitions; still less of suggesting, amid all the vertiginously proliferating and often contradictory senses assigned to the word, that one or another is in some way original or primary. Nor shall I attempt to lay claim to some universal validity for what is after all both a relatively recent and a rather local addition to the lexicon; or to suggest that recognisably humanistic developments cast in an entirely different dialect (the Confucian *jen*, for example, or the *al-adab* of medieval Islam) have less interest or relevance for western readers. The book will not be much concerned with the various organisations, such as the Humanist Association and the National Secular Society, that promote a set of secularist beliefs and commitments as an alternative to Christianity, in a language and with a contentious assurance that declare their Victorian pedigree and, often, their indifference or hostility to the deeper and more troubled implications of the idea. They are easy enough to find (try googling *humanism* or *secularism*) and need no additional publicity from me. Least of all shall I be launching yet another knockabout polemic on the crimes and follies of orga-nised religion, a currently popular genre already staked out by Richard Dawkins and Christopher Hitchens, the Don Quixote and Sancho Panza of 'secular fundamentalism', before whose armour-plated certainties Humpty himself might flinch (Daw-kins 2006; Hitchens 2007).

The purpose of this book is rather to explore the origin and history of the concept of humanism, the uses to which it has been put in different times and contexts, the questions it has tried to answer, the flags of convenience under which it has sailed; and above all to suggest what might be 'at stake', historically and ideolo-gically, in the often bitter contentions in which it has taken on such an array of competing significations and values. It might be argued, indeed, that the book should be titled 'Humanisms', to avoid any implication that its subject is a singular, stable entity. For the meanings of a powerful and complex word are never simply definitions, never a matter for lexicography alone. They are tied inescapably to the linguistic and cultural *authority* (real, absent, wished-for or fought over) of those who use it. The important question, over and above what the word *means* in a particular context, is why and how that meaning *matters*, and for whom. On this at least, Humpty Dumpty's advice cannot be improved on by the cultural historian. When Alice wonders, innocently, 'whether you *can* make words mean so many different things', the philosophical egg goes straight to the heart of the matter: '"The question is," said Humpty Dumpty, "which is to be master – that's all."'

The sequence of the chapters that follow – the first two deal-ing with the nineteenth and twentieth centuries, the third and fourth with the period from the fifteenth to the later eighteenth century, while the fifth goes back still further, to the early ety-mology of the word 'human' and its uses in antiquity – may look eccentric; and it might seem that a reader hoping for a straight-forward chronological narrative would do better to start at the end, then read chapters 3 and 4, before turning back finally to the first two. Feel free to do that if you wish. But the order of the first four chapters, ending where they began in the tumultuous half century that separates Immanuel Kant's 'Enlightenment' essay from the educational reforms of Wilhelm von Humboldt, the secession of the North American colonies from the fall of Napoleon, does have its own peculiar logic, which I hope will be apparent to the reader who is patient enough to let it unfold in its own way – by which time the reason for leaving the beginning until the end may also have become a bit clearer.

1

THE INVENTION OF HUMANITY

To be radical is to grasp things by the root. But for man the root is man himself.

(Karl Marx)

The Parthenon, the ancient temple of the warrior-goddess Athena that dominates the limestone crag of the Acropolis in Athens, is certainly one of the most photographed buildings in the world. But among the innumerable snapshots of that famous ruin there is one in particular that haunts the memory. In the background stands the eastern facade of the great temple, its eight Doric columns and broken pediment catching the early sun, with the Athenian suburbs and the Aegalean hills faintly visible in the haze to the west. In the foreground, on a circular floor that once supported a temple consecrated to the Roman emperor Augustus, a dozen men in uniform are standing around a makeshift flagpole, up which a large flag, swelling gently in the morning breeze, is being raised. Over the centuries many soldiers – Persians, Spartans, Macedonians, Romans, Goths, Byzantines, Franks, Catalans, Venetians, Ottomans, Bavarians – have stood on that spot. But this is different. The date is 27

April 1941; the soldiers wear the uniform of the sixth armoured division of the German *Wehrmacht*; and the flag that billows above the occupied city bears the insignia of Adolf Hitler's would-be thousand-year Third Reich, the *Hakenkreuz* or swastika (Bullock 1985: 174).

For most people to whom it means anything at all, the photograph probably records one of the elemental confrontations of the modern period: on the one hand, the Parthenon, supreme symbol of Athens and the wider Hellenic world, the 'cradle of civilisation', the birthplace of democracy (the very word is Athenian) and rationality, the unsurpassable paradigm of human beauty and wisdom; on the other, the despotic savagery and irrationality of the Third Reich, a new barbarism of blood and iron. The twentieth century, for all its later horrors, produced none to equal those that came out of Germany between 1933 and 1945; and the cool Pentelic marble whose stupendous symmetries have witnessed and survived so many conquering empires here submits to the latest and most terrible of them all. It is as if Matthew Arnold's worst nightmare, the final overthrow of culture, with its Hellenic 'sweetness and light', by the 'ignorant armies' of anarchy and darkness, has taken concrete form on that spring morning in 1941.

But although photographs never lie, that may only be because they never say anything unequivocal at all. Interpretation is everything; and a little digging can always yield another reading. The part-time secretary of the small Nazi Party organisation in Athens was the forty-one-year-old Walter Wrede, who worked as a classical archaeologist at the German Archaeological School in the city. For Wrede, 27 April was a big day, rich compensation for the months of anti-German abuse that had driven him to take up almost permanent refuge in the School. Wrede it was who had the honour of meeting the advance party of the occupying sixth division when they drove into the city that morning and conducting them in person to the Acropolis. Later he posed for photographs with Field-Marshal Brauchitsch, General von Stumme and other staff officers, ardent Nazis every one of them, and, like most middle-class Germans, enthusiastic philhellenes. All Germans, wrote General Lanz, 'admire the great past and lofty culture of Hellas' (Mazower 1993: 158). Hitler himself, in a letter to his ally Benito Mussolini, recorded with pride this epochal encounter between a resurgent Germany and the 'symbol of modern culture' (Mazower 1993: 8). Had not the great Richard Wagner, Teutonic nationalist and anti-Semite, been acclaimed by his disciple Friedrich Nietzsche as the contemporary incarnation of the Hellenic spirit? Was not the very notion of the 'Aryan' type, so central to the National Socialist doctrine of racial purity, borrowed from the work of the German philologists and Hellenists of the previous century (Bernal 1987: 330–36)? Had not the Nazi philosopher Martin Heidegger only the other day hailed Greek civilisation as 'the beginning of our spiritual-historical being', a destiny which 'awaits us, as a distant command bidding us catch up with its greatness' (Guignan 1993: 32)? And as for the *Führer* himself, had he not declared that, amidst all the trash and filth produced by degenerate races through the ages, the only authentic artistic heritage was the Greco-German? From one point of view, at least, that sunny morning in 1941 witnessed not a tragic confrontation between Hellenic culture and barbaric anarchy, but the historic affirmation of an ancient continuity, in which the invading Germans appear not as the destroyers of Greek civilisation but as its liberators, the heirs and custodians of its sacred flame.

So many stories, wrote Bertolt Brecht, so many questions. But what has all this to do with *humanism*? Well firstly, as we have already seen, the word itself is of German coinage; and secondly, its credentials are Greek. *Humanismus* was a term devised, probably by the educationalist Friedrich Immanuel Niethammer, in the early nineteenth century to describe a high-school and university curriculum based on what had been known since the Middle Ages as the 'humanities': the study of ancient Greek and Latin, and of the literature, history and culture of the peoples who spoke them. The word was soon taken up by cultural historians like Georg Voigt and Jacob Burckhardt to describe the humanistic 'new learning', a 'Renaissance' or rebirth of Greco-Roman civilisation and its associated values promoted by the *umanisti* or professional teachers and scholars in fifteenth-century Italy. And since the notion of the Renaissance, and with it a whole way of thinking about the relations between past and present, antiquity and modernity, continues in its turn to exert an enduring influence, these early nineteenth-century German debates about education and culture, history and politics, will repay a closer look.

ROMANTIC HUMANISM

The neo-humanistic (*neuhumanistisch*) syllabus pioneered by educational reformers like Niethammer, along with better-known contemporaries like the philosopher G.W.F. Hegel and Wilhelm von Humboldt, creator of the modern *Gymnasium* (high school) system and founder of the University of Berlin, was an attempt to civilise the crudely practical and chauvinistic (the poet Heinrich Heine called it *philister*, 'philistine') ethos of the North German ruling and middle classes. Like the Florentine *umanisti* from whom they borrowed their watchword, the German reformers of the early nineteenth century grounded their curriculum in 'classics': Latin and, especially, Greek language, literature and culture, refracted through the romantic Hellenism of the art historian Winckelmann and the poets Goethe and Hölderlin. 'Our study of Greek history', wrote Humboldt,

is a matter quite different from our other studies ... Knowledge of the Greeks is not merely pleasant, useful or necessary to us – no, in the Greeks alone we find the ideal of what we should like to be and produce.

(Bernal 1987: 287)

And in the same spirit, the curriculum of Hegel's *Egidium Gymnasium* in Nuremberg gave due weight to mathematics, history and physical education; but half of its twenty-seven hours of weekly instruction were devoted to the study of Greek and Latin.

The Hellenism of these neo-humanist educators was as far from the reactionary pedantry of Oxford 'classics' as it was from the merely ornamental neoclassicism of so much post-Renaissance English poetry, of the kind that Samuel Johnson dismissed contemptuously as a 'train of mythological imagery such as a college easily supplies' (Johnson 1906). The Hellenic ideal belonged, for Hegel and Humboldt as for Goethe and Schiller, not to the remote past and the post-mortem formalities of an ancient language, but to the future. For them, the modern Germany they were engaged in building, cultured, orderly and rational, would be a modern-day Hellas, the fruition of what the ancient Greeks had dreamed. 'The name of Greece', Hegel wrote, 'strikes home to the hearts of men of education in Europe, and more particularly is this so with us Germans' (Bernal 1987: 295). And his most famous and most insubordinate disciple inherited his Hellenism, if not his enthusiasm for the authoritarian ethos of the Prussian state. 'Man's self-esteem,' wrote the young Karl Marx in 1843,

> his sense of freedom, must be awakened in the breast of [the German] people. This sense vanished from the world with the Greeks, and with Christianity it took up residence in the blue mists of heaven, but only with its aid can society ever again become a community of men that can fulfil their highest needs, a democratic state.
>
> (Marx 1975: 201)

Marx himself was soon to turn sharply against the Hegelian idealism of supposing that people's lives can be transformed simply by reawakening the passion for freedom in their heads and hearts. Already by 1844 he was formulating a radical humanism ('to be radical is to grasp things by the root. But for man the root is man himself.') based not on the speculative abstraction of Hegelian logic but on the dynamic identity of man and nature, revealed in 'the inexhaustible, vital, sensuous, concrete activity' of human labour:

> *Communism* is the *positive* supersession of *private property* as *human self estrangement*, and hence the true *appropriation* of the *human* essence through and for man; it is the complete restoration of man to himself as a *social*, i.e. human, being ... This communism, as fully developed naturalism, equals humanism, and as fully developed humanism equals naturalism; it is the *genuine* resolution of the

conflict between man and nature, and between man and man, the true resolution of the conflict between existence and being, between objectification and self-affirmation, between freedom and necessity, between individual and species. It is the solution of the riddle of history and knows itself to be the solution.

(Marx 1975: 348)

Later still, after the revolutionary hopes of 1848–9 have been dashed, this vein of utopian enthusiasm will be submitted in its turn to the astringent discipline of historical actuality. But the fascination with ancient Greece, the sense that it represents a still-unfulfilled ideal, persists. In an early draft of the work that will become *Das Kapital*, Marx has been arguing that Greek art can only be understood in the context of the social relations and conditions that produced it, a 'Marxist' commonplace that is hardly likely to arouse much argument even today. 'But the difficulty', he continues,

lies not in understanding that the Greek arts and epic are bound up with certain forms of social development. The difficulty is that they still afford us artistic pleasure and that in a certain respect they count as a norm and as an unattainable model.

(Marx 1973a: 111)

The ancient Greeks, he suggests, represent 'the historic childhood of humanity'; and although 'a man cannot become a child again', he can still 'find joy in the child's naïveté', and even 'strive to reproduce its truth at a higher stage'.

The veteran theorist of class struggle understood perfectly well, of course, that Athenian democracy was built with bricks of slavery, and cemented with a xenophobic contempt for non-Greek-speaking 'barbarians' as virulent as the jingoism of any Tory imperialist; but for the moment, caught in the potent enchantment of the old temple on its rock, he had forgotten. The passage, written in London in 1857, the year of the Indian 'Mutiny' and the British seizure of Canton, suggests how deeply even the most radical thought of the period was saturated by the Hellenocentric ideals of Goethean romanticism and Humboldtian *Humanismus*.

1857, the year in which Marx wrote the unpublished *Grundrisse*, is also, as it happens, the year of *Tom Brown's Schooldays*. The humanist ethos had already found its way into British intellectual culture through the advocacy of Germanophiles like Samuel Coleridge, his disciple Connop Thirlwall, whose massive *History of Greece* was an early monument to the influence in England of German classical scholarship, and Thomas Arnold. Arnold above all, through his innovative regime as headmaster of Rugby School, established the now-familiar public school curriculum, with its twin pillars of classics and competitive games (the second no less 'Hellenic' in inspiration than the first), that continues to dominate the education of the English ruling class to the present day. And Dr Arnold's most famous and influential pupil, we may guess, was not his son Matthew, enthusiastic Goethean and energetic propagandist for a culture of Hellenic 'sweetness and light' to redeem the philistinism of the propertied classes and the looming anarchy of capitalist class war, but his fictional contemporary Tom Brown, whose Rugby schooldays, as described in Thomas Hughes' idyllically nostalgic narrative, did more than anything else in the period to establish Arnold's peculiarly English hybrid of German *Bildung* and British heartiness in the popular imagination. In one particularly poignant scene, Tom and his friend Arthur, waiting their turn to bat against a visiting eleven, are discussing with a young master the importance of grasping the finer points of Greek syntax. Out on the pitch a skilful stroke is played, to applause.

> 'How well they are bowling, though,' said Arthur, 'they don't mean to be beat, I can see.'
>
> 'There now,' struck in the master, 'you see that's just what I have been preaching this half-hour. The delicate play is the true thing. I don't understand cricket, so I don't enjoy those fine draws which you tell me are the best play, though when you or Raggles hit a hard ball away for six I am as delighted as anyone. Don't you see the analogy?'
>
> 'Yes, sir,' answered Tom, looking up, roguishly, 'I see; only the question remains whether I should have got most good by

understanding Greek particles or cricket thoroughly. I'm such a thick, I never should have had time for both.'

'I see you are an incorrigible,' said the master with a chuckle, 'but I refute you by an example. Arthur there has taken in Greek and cricket too.'

(Hughes 1989: 353)

'We are all Greeks': Shelley's words might serve as a motto for generations of young middle-class Englishmen – English *men*, since the Hellenic ideal, like the public schools themselves, is overwhelmingly male territory. From the champions of Greek independence in the 1820s like Shelley's friend Byron, to the officers who sent their troops into combat in the 1915 Dardanelles campaign with lines from Homer's *Iliad* ringing in their ears, they modelled their ideas of conduct on an improbable but potent compound of the Trojan War and the Varsity match, epic poetry and the laws of cricket and rugby (the latter a version of football reputedly invented at Arnold's school). Few if any would have called themselves 'humanists', a word that in England carried uncomfortable connotations of Unitarianism or even downright atheism, and was certainly incompatible with the profession of Christian and gentleman (Hughes himself was a Christian Socialist). But all were the legitimate offspring of *Humanismus* nonetheless, translated into an English cultural register, to be sure, but still bearing the unmistakable features of its Prussian and romantic lineage.

RENAISSANCE MAN: A NINETEENTH-CENTURY CREATION

Jacob Burckhardt, a German-speaking Swiss and himself a devoted child of the same tradition, defined humanism as 'the discovery of the world and of man'; but this was a humanism whose roots lay not in the ancient Greece of Winckelmann and Humboldt but in the city-states of fifteenth-century Italy. His central historical question, the same question posed by other social thinkers like Karl Marx and Max Weber, was about the conditions that made possible, or inevitable, the bourgeois revolution of modernity. Why, they asked, did the characteristic features of modern liberal capitalism, dynamic, innovative and expansive, develop in Europe and North America rather than in the ancient societies, no less elaborate in culture or technology, of Asia and the Orient? Marx found his explanation in the expansion of merchant capital and the emergence of a class of ambitious burghers in late-medieval towns. Weber located his in the frugal domestic economy and Calvinist independence of the Protestant middle classes in post-reformation Europe (Weber 1930). For Burckhardt the explanation lay in a particular interplay between the political and military necessities of independent Italian cities and the secular individualism, nurtured by a humanist interest in antiquity but essentially quite new, of their middle-class citizenry and its rulers. This is the theme of his best-known and most influential work, *The Civilisation of the Renaissance in Italy*, published in 1860.

Germany in Burckhardt's time was evolving painfully from an agglomeration of small principalities towards a unified national state; and the title he gave to the first part of the work, 'The State as a Work of Art', spoke to contemporary preoccupations with statehood and national unity. Emergent Germany found her reflection and inspiration here in the writings of Renaissance humanist historians, political theorists and jurists like Guiccardini, Machiavelli, Grotius and Bodin, and in the embattled but fiercely independent states like Florence and Geneva in and about which they wrote. Behind all these, still, stood the unsurpassable paradigm of Periclean Athens, supreme instance of 'the state determined by culture', the city of which Burckhardt remarked wistfully that, alone in world history, she 'has no tedious pages' (Burckhardt 1964: 217–18). But the Greek ideal of humane civilisation, glimpsed briefly in the charmed interim between the Persian and the Peloponnesian wars, and in the writings of the Athenian poets and philosophers, was no more than the seed from which the great oak of German culture would rise.

Above all, Burckhardt's Renaissance was the epoch of the *individual*. The second part of his great work is titled 'The Development of the Individual'; and the concept, the central one in his understanding of the period, denotes not just those heroic or demonic *uomini universali*, the gifted, brutal Sforzas, Borgias and Medicis who haunt the popular histories of the period, but the development of a universal capacity to think of yourself, in a fundamental way, as a free and unique being: not as Florentine or Marseillais or a sailor or Roman Catholic or somebody's daughter or grandson, important though all those affiliations might be, but as a free-standing self-determining person with an identity and a name that is not simply a marker of family, birthplace or occupation but is 'proper', that is, belonging to you alone.

Burckhardt does not comment, though it would not contradict his argument, on the modernity of many of the key terms in that last sentence: *individual*, *identity*, *proper*. Nor does he remark on the striking semantic reversals that from the sixteenth century had already, when he wrote, rendered words like *individual* (originally 'inseparable') and *identity* ('sameness') over to meanings almost exactly the opposite of their traditional ones. His interest is in the political significance of Renaissance individualism, portending the end of medieval society, with its supposedly inert aggregations of nameless, unselfconscious subjects, and the onset of the modern nation state, populated and animated by individual citizens.

Burckhardt is able, of course, to support his reading of the Renaissance from the writings of the period, which certainly exhibit a fascination with heroic individuality: Machiavelli's ruthlessly success-oriented *Prince*, Giorgio Vasari's *Lives of the Painters*, the outrageous egoists and megalomaniacs of Marlowe's tragedies. But it is equally easy to see that 'individualism' itself is a modern concern, a product of the period that produced Samuel Smiles' *Self Help* (1859, soon followed by *Character*, *Thrift* and *Duty*) and the ethos of manly independence forged by the public school. The desire to find in the fifteenth and sixteenth centuries the headwaters of an essentially nineteenth-century individuality manifests itself even more dramatically in a historical extravaganza called *The Renaissance* (1877) by the French diplomat and royalist Arthur, Comte de Gobineau; but whereas Burckhardt's Renaissance exhibits a tumultuous dialectic between individual energies, political or artistic, and the necessary synergy of state and citizenry, Gobineau's account of the period, which takes the form of a series of dialogues between famous Italians like Michelangelo, Savonarola and Cesare Borgia, finds in it not civic solidarity and the first stirrings of modern statecraft but the uncompromising selfhood and will to power of individual 'genius', the expression of an innate superiority:

> the great law of the world ... is to live, to enlarge and develop our most active and sublime qualities, in such a way that from any sphere we can always strive to reach one that is wider, more airy, more elevated ... Leave weakness and scruples to the petty minds and the rabble of underlings.
>
> (Gobineau 1970: 199–200)

This proto-Nietzschean inclination leads to some painful contortions, as does his infatuation with the Teutonic 'race' and 'blood' and his contempt for the degenerate Mediterranean peoples, which requires him, absurdly, to conscript Michelangelo, the Borgias and other Renaissance supermen as honorary Germans. According to Gobineau, the Renaissance, that 'magnificent flowering of artistic and literary culture' in which we witness 'the flower of the human spirit most vividly in bloom', is entirely the result of the energising enrichment of Roman with Teutonic blood; an efflorescence all too tragically brief, as Italy falls back into its habitual racial torpor: 'its glory scarcely lasted a hundred years and, when it had ended, the general agony began again' (Gobineau 1970: 149).

Such vapid invocations to 'the flower of the human spirit' remind us that this, too, is a variety of humanism, of a kind that does not encourage complacency. From the Germanophile Gobineau, who fantasised his own quite spurious Teutonic ancestry and is best known now for his *Essay on the Inequality of Human Races* (1853), the trail leads, via friendship with the admiring Richard Wagner and the enthusiastic approval of Nietzsche's fanatical sister Elizabeth, more or less directly to those *Wehrmacht* officers and Nazi functionaries on the Acropolis in 1941. He too, naturally, was a philhellene, and the *Essay*, in which the ancient Greeks are contrasted with the degenerate Romans as bearers of the pure Aryan blood-line, was a standard school-text in Hitler's Germany.

For all their differences – and I do not mean for a moment to suggest any sympathy of aims or temperament between the retiring, scholarly Burckhardt and the vain, self-aggrandising Gobineau – the important thing for both writers is the historical role of Renaissance humanism in instituting a new and distinctively modern notion of human individuality, a notion projected back onto the writings of fifteenth- and sixteenth-century *umanisti*, but demonstrably shaped by and inseparable from nineteenth-century conditions and concerns. The political energies and instabilities unleashed by the American and French revolutions of the previous century; the explosive acceleration of capitalist production, with its spectral antagonist, the industrial working class; the expansion of the great European nation states, in the competitive scramble for economic and political hegemony, into imperial powers with a vast extramural proletariat of subjugated peoples; the dilapidation of Christianity as a resource of moral authority and national ideology: all these familiar features of nineteenth-century experience necessitated an idea that could at once rationalise an explosive and unpredictable modernity (as the triumphant achievement of heroic human endeavour) and justify or palliate its all-too-visible brutalities and inequalities.

Clearly a concept capable of bearing such a weight of explanatory responsibility will be fraught with contradictory meanings and implications. For Gobineau, humanism dictates the racial superiority of the Teuton and the unaccountable mastery of individual genius. For the young Marx it underwrites the necessity of revolution and the dream of a humanity emancipated from inequality and exploitation. Matthew Arnold invokes an eirenic humanistic 'culture' to arbitrate and unify the divisive anarchy of politics and class; while freethinkers like T.H. Huxley, the champion of 'godless' Darwinism who coined the word 'agnostic', and Charles Bradlaugh, founder of the National Secular Society, summon the spirit of humanism to cast out the last tenacious delusions of Christian superstition.

Different and clearly incompatible versions of the 'human' are circulating here, within the orbit of a single concept. For Arnold, the 'central ... truly human point of view', though evidently modern and European, stands for something essential, above and beyond the accidents of historical or national difference, a quality sometimes eclipsed by ignorance or self-interest, but visible in Homer and Sophocles no less than in Shakespeare or Goethe twenty or more centuries later; whereas for Marx the 'human' is not a single unchanging entity at all but a sign of change, the site of a continuous transformation. What they share – what makes them all 'humanists' – is their conviction of the unwavering centrality of the 'human' itself.

THE BIRTH OF MODERNITY

The reference to a 'central, a truly human point of view' comes from Arnold's discussion of Chaucer in an essay called 'The Study of Poetry' in the 1888 *Essays in Criticism*, and it serves as a useful starting-point for an exploration of the English appropriation of Burckhardtian *Humanismus*. Arnold has been discussing the peculiar limitations of medieval romance poetry, the *Song of Roland*, the *Romance of the Rose*, the Arthurian tales and troubadour lyrics, with their narrow range of subject-matter and attitude, their uncritical deference to social and religious orthodoxy. Then in the fourteenth century 'there comes an Englishman nourished on this poetry', but something has changed:

> If we ask ourselves wherein consists the immense superiority of Chaucer's poetry over the romance poetry – why it is that in passing from this to Chaucer we suddenly feel ourselves to be in another world – we shall find that his superiority is both in the substance of his poetry and in the style of his poetry. His superiority in substance is given by his large, free, simple, clear yet kindly view of human life, – so unlike the total want, in the romance-poets, of all intelligent command of it. Chaucer has not their helplessness; he has gained the power to survey the world from a central, a truly human point of view.
>
> (Arnold 1888: 27–28)

This description of Chaucer's poetry may seem uncontentious enough, perhaps even a bit banal. Who would want to deny that the *Canterbury Tales* and *Troilus and Criseyde*, with their stories of men and women meeting, marrying, quarrelling, falling in and out of love, are written from a 'human point of view'? But why the insistence that that point of view is 'central'? And what is implied by the special emphasis suggested by *truly* human'? What other points of view, eccentric, marginal or inauthentic, are implied in its coupling of the true, the central and the human?

The key stress, clearly, falls on the *human*, a word Arnold uses in a way that carries a number of powerful implications. One is historical. Chaucer, for Arnold, is the first modern, the first English writer to see the world not, like his medieval forebears and contemporaries (in this case the writers of medieval French romances), *sub specie aeternitatis*, from the cosmic vantage of a transcendent wisdom and authority embodied in the doctrines and traditions of the Church, still less from the parochial view-point of a particular social group (the aristocracy) or professional élite (monks or troubadours), but through the everyday experience of ordinary human beings, of all classes and both sexes. In his writing, the passage suggests, we encounter for the first time the authentic ('truly human') voice of secular individuality: not some solemn choreography of allegorical Everyman and Every-woman acting out a bloodless theological paradigm, but what Arnold's contemporary Thomas Hardy called 'real enactments of the intensest kind': people with recognisable names and real occupations meeting and parting, fighting and loving in places whose names you can actually find on a map.

The second implication is ethical. Chaucer, we are invited to conclude, is not only an ordinary human being like ourselves, but also a great poet. All those idiomatic characters with their quirky individuality are gathered into the generously encom-passing ('central') humanity of the poet himself, who views them not as the playthings of an inscrutable deity but as fellow crea-tures, citizens like himself, with the common human frailties and aspirations. Thus Chaucer's humanity, for Arnold, is both general and special, common and rare. Each of us lives our human-ness as a uniquely individual experience; but that experience, we are asked to feel, is part of a larger, all-embracing humanity, a 'human condition', to which the great poets of the European tradition, Homer and Dante and Chaucer and Shakespeare and Milton and Goethe, can give us the key. In this sense, evidently, Arnold's 'central ... truly human point of view' is not really – or not only – a historical matter at all, but an appeal to the essentially, universally human.

What, if anything, all this has to do with what the historical Geoffrey Chaucer actually wrote (or thought) is, for our purposes, neither here nor there. What is clear is that Arnold's Chaucer is himself a character in what the French philosopher of the 'postmodern' Jean-François Lyotard (1984) calls a 'metanarrative', a potent historical and ideological *myth*; and that myth (I use the word to signify not a primitive fiction or delusion but a strong and enduring story) is most certainly both here and there: *there* in the late nineteenth century, where this particularly powerful and complex notion of the 'human' – a quality at once local and universal, historical and timeless – first finds its full articulation, and *here* too, a hundred and twenty years later, in the twenty-first, where, whether or not we care about or have even heard of Geoffrey Chaucer or Matthew Arnold, it continues to shape not just the identity and subjectivity but the practical existence of a large proportion of the people, and the peoples, of the world. It is the myth of the *modern*; the *Renaissance* is its infancy; and its guiding ethos, its watchword, is *humanism*.

***

The essence of humanism consisted in a new and vital perception of the dignity of man as a rational being apart from theological determinations, and in the further perception that classic literature alone displayed human nature in the plenitude of intellectual and moral freedom. It was partly a reaction against ecclesiastical despotism, partly an attempt to find the point of unity for all that had been thought and done by man, within the mind restored to consciousness of its own sovereign faculty.

(Symonds 1898: 52)

The second volume of J.A. Symonds' *The Renaissance in Italy*, subtitled *The Revival of Learning* and first published in 1877, three years before Arnold's 'The Study of Poetry', did more than any other book to establish for English readers the Burckhardtian historiography of the Renaissance, and the centrality to it of humanism. For Symonds, as for Arnold, the recovery by the scholars, poets and painters of the fourteenth and fifteenth centuries not just of the writings but with them the spirit of classical antiquity is an achievement not of antiquarianism but, in the highest degree, of heroic modernity, nothing less than the foundation of a new humanity. Symonds called Chaucer's older contemporary, the Italian scholar-poet Francesco Petrarca (Petrarch), 'the Columbus of a new spiritual hemisphere, the discoverer of modern culture'; and of the students of the Byzantine humanist Manolis Chrysoloras he wrote that they

> felt that the Greek texts, whereof he alone supplied the key, contained those elements of spiritual freedom and intellectual culture without which the civilisation of the modern world would be impossible ... The study of Greek implied the birth of criticism, comparison, research. Systems based on ignorance and superstition were destined to give way before it. The study of Greek opened philosophical horizons far beyond the dreamworld of the churchmen and the monks; it stimulated the germs of science, suggested new astronomical hypotheses, and indirectly led to the discovery of America ... we are justified in regarding the point of contact between the Greek teacher Chrysoloras and his Florentine pupils as one of the most momentous crises in the history of civilisation.
>
> (Symonds 1898: 81–82)

Momentous indeed, if from that Tuscan schoolroom flowed not only the colonisation of the Americas, named after the sixteenth-century Florentine adventurer Amerigo Vespucci, but also the imperial destinies of nineteenth-century Germany, France and, supremely, Great Britain. Symonds' formulation of these connections, with their powerful legitimation of the imperialist enterprise, is admirably uncomplicated:

> Such is the *Lampadephoria*, or torch-race, of the nations. Greece stretches forth her hand to Italy; Italy consigns the fire to Northern

Europe; the people of the North pass on the flame to America, to India, and the Australasian isles.

(Symonds 1898: 399)

Symonds and Arnold, then, give popular currency in England to ideas, including the idea of humanism itself, first articulated by German-speaking historians and philosophers a generation earlier: ideas developed within a distinctively German tradition and at a particularly critical moment in the historical and cultural formation of modern Germany. But can a word capable of sustaining so many and so diverse a variety of uses be said to mean anything at all? Is it any more than a blank screen onto which anyone can project their flickering fantasies of power or happiness? It may be, of course, that it is precisely this protean adaptability and serviceable vagueness that gives the word its rhetorical power and range. For in these nineteenth-century discourses, the figure of the human, though deployed in contexts that might suggest that it is geographically and historically specific, in reality signifies something that is everywhere and always the same. Burckhardt, we have seen, credited the Italian humanists with the 'discovery of the world and man', a phrase that conceives of 'man' as a continent, like the undiscovered Indies or the New World, awaiting its Vasco da Gama or Columbus; while Symonds praised Petrarch and his successors for the realisation that 'classic literature alone displayed human nature in the plenitude of intellectual and moral freedom'. We might call this the myth of essential and universal Man: essential, because humanity – human-ness – is the inseparable and central essence, the defining quality, of human beings; universal, because that essential humanity is shared by all human beings, of whatever time or place.

To the extent that such formulations of the 'human' would have appeared strange, perhaps unintelligible, and almost certainly blasphemously presumptuous to those earlier humanists who are credited with its 'discovery', 'Renaissance humanism', expressive of an essential humanity unconditioned by time, place or circumstance, is a nineteenth-century anachronism. But it is an anachronism that is still deeply engrained in contemporary self-consciousness and everyday common sense, so deeply that it requires a conscious effort, every time someone appeals to 'human nature' or 'the human condition', to recall how recent such notions are, how specific to a particular history, location and point of view, and how very odd it would seem, in cultures historically or ethnologically unlike our own, to separate out and privilege 'Man' in this way.

THE RELIGION OF HUMANITY

Where, then, if not from the scholarly humanists of fifteenth-century Italy, does this abstract humanism, with its universalist and essentialist conception of Man, come from? In its origins, it is a political rather than a philosophical notion, deriving from the revolutionary discourse of rights. When Rousseau announces in *The Social Contract* (1762) that '*L'homme est né libre, et par-tout il est dans les fers*' ('Man is born free, but is everywhere in chains'), the concept already enfolds a distinction between an abstract 'Man', defined by an essential freedom, and actual 'men' caught in the toils of historical servitude. The 'Rights of Man' announced by Thomas Paine in his famous polemic of that name in 1792 belong not to this or that group of 'men' but to 'Man' in general. Indeed, we might say that it is precisely in the move from the 'empirical plurality' of an earlier republicanism – from, say, the 'all men naturally were born free' of John Milton's *Tenure of Kings and Magistrates* (1649) or the 'self-evident truth' that 'all men are created equal' of Thomas Jefferson's *Declaration of Independence* (1776) – to the abstract singularity and universality of Rousseau's and Paine's 'Man' that, as we shall see, a full-blown essentialist humanism is generated.

Of course, 'universality' is a tricky notion, and universals may not always be quite as generously inclusive as they would have us suppose. Jefferson, like all his wealthy neighbours, owned domestic slaves, though with a troubled conscience, and the denunciation of the 'execrable commerce' that he included in the first draft of the Declaration was struck out by the Congress 'in complaisance to South Carolina and Georgia'. Mary Wollstonecraft's response to Paine (and to his *bête noire*, Edmund Burke) was to issue a *Vindication of the Rights of Woman* (1792) that his own book appeared to have overlooked. And Karl Marx pointed out that the heady rhetoric of 'Universal Man' that accompanied the revolutions of the eighteenth and nineteenth centuries tended to give way, once its ideological work was done, to the promotion of a rather narrower and more pragmatic set of class interests (Marx 1973b: 148–50). One of the effects of a universalising notion like 'Man' is to dissolve precisely such particularities as race, sex and class; and for that reason it is always prudent to ask what specific historical and local interests may be at work within grandly ecumenical notions like Symonds' 'point of unity for all that had been thought and done by man' or Arnold's 'central ... truly human point of view': what the later nineteenth century dubbed, in lieu of the Christianity in which it could no longer believe, the 'religion of humanity'.

The phrase 'religion of humanity' was coined by Thomas Paine in a letter 'To the People of England, Nov 21 1778', reprinted in *The American Crisis* (1780). The passage has a painful contemporary relevance.

> The arm of Britain has been spoken of as the arm of the Almighty, and she has lived of late as if she thought the whole world created for her diversion. Her politics, instead of civilizing, has tended to brutalize mankind, and under the vain, unmeaning title of "Defender of the Faith," she has made war like an Indian against the religion of humanity.

Paine called himself a 'theophilanthropist', a word combining the Greek words for 'God', 'love' and 'man', and indicating that while he believed in the existence of a creating intelligence in the universe, he entirely rejected the claims made by and for all existing religious doctrines, especially their miraculous, transcendental and salvationist pretensions. The Parisian 'Society of Theophilanthropy' which he sponsored, and whose inaugural address he gave in 1797, is described by his biographer as 'a forerunner of the ethical and humanist societies that proliferated later' (Williamson 1973: 236); and the trenchantly witty *Age of Reason* (1793), which enraged the respectable even more than *The*

Rights of Man had done, pours scorn on the supernatural impos-
tures of scripture, combining Voltairean mockery with Paine's
own style of taproom ridicule to expose the absurdity of a
theology built on a collection of incoherent Levantine folktales.

The Age of Reason forms a link between what Lyotard (1984:
31) calls 'the two major versions of the narrative of legitimation':
the abstractly rationalistic critique of the eighteenth-century
philosophes and the radical historical theology, no less destructive
of traditional pieties, of nineteenth-century biblical scholars like
David Friedrich Strauss and his younger English contemporary
Charles Hennell. The first is political, largely French in inspiration, and projects 'humanity as the hero of liberty'. The second is
philosophical, German, seeks the totality and autonomy of
knowledge, and stresses *understanding* rather than *freedom* as the
key to human fulfilment and emancipation. The two themes
converge and compete in complex ways throughout the nineteenth century and beyond, and between them set the parameters
of its various humanisms. It was a reading of Hennell's *Inquiry
into the Origins of Christianity* (1838) that helped a young writer
called Mary Ann Evans to articulate her own increasingly sceptical ideas about official Christianity, ideas she was to develop
more fully in translations of Strauss' *Das Leben Jesu* (*The Life of
Jesus*, 1846) and Ludwig Feuerbach's ardently Hegelian *Das Wesen
des Christentums* (*The Essence of Christianity*, 1854), and finally, as
'George Eliot', in a series of novels informed by her conviction
that

> the fellowship between man and man which has been the principle of
> development, social and moral, is not dependent on conceptions of
> what is not man ... the idea of God, so far as it has been a high
> spiritual influence, is the ideal of a goodness entirely human (i.e. an
> exaltation of the human).

> (Haight 1954–5: 98)

The idea that 'God' is simply the projection or externalisation of
as yet unrealised human qualities and aspirations indicates the
degree to which the young George Eliot's thinking was shaped
by the romantic humanism of Feuerbach's *'homo homini deus est'*

('man is god to man', or 'god is [nothing other than] man to himself'). But the writer who supplied the most systematic account of a secular 'religion of humanity', and who gave it for a while a currency and controversial immediacy to rival anything by Marx or Darwin, was the French 'positivist' Auguste Comte. A universe without supernatural sanction or presence, Comte argued, can be fully understood only by the scientific description of 'positive' phenomena, stripped of the sentimental pieties of traditional religion or romantic pantheism. As for human beings in that godless universe, their moral and social coexistence has no basis to appeal to beyond their own resources of sympathetic fellow-feeling, resources that are themselves the result of the evolutionary development of the species. 'The human heart', George Eliot herself wrote in her Comtean poem 'The Spanish Gypsy', 'Finds nowhere shelter but in human kind'.

Comte himself argued in his *Système de politique positive* (1851–4) for the construction of an atheistic religion (*culte*) founded on humanist principles, complete with doctrines and liturgy; and although George Eliot had reservations about Comte, and remained uncommitted to the final systematisation of his ideas, she warmly endorsed the project of an ethical religion designed to occupy the place vacated by a discredited Christianity. This is the 'religion of humanity' that so engrossed positivists like her partner G.H. Lewes and their friend Frederic Harrison, who in 1877 wrote urging her to state publicly 'your judgement of a Religion of Humanity as a possible rallying point for mankind in the future', appealing especially on behalf of those half-hearted Comteans like herself 'who reject it [the merciless rigour of the *Système*, recently translated by Harriet Martineau] in different degrees but converge to the general idea of Humanity, as the ultimate centre of life and of thought' (Haight 1968: 506).

Her hesitation is not difficult to understand. If Comte dismantles the institutional and liturgical apparatus of Catholic Christianity, he puts in its place a set of structures and observances every bit as rigid and elaborate. Comte's secular religion is no vague effusion of benevolent humanist piety, but a complete system of belief and ritual, with liturgy and sacraments, priesthood and pontiff, all organised around the public veneration of

Humanity, the *Grand Etre* (Great Being), later to be supplemented in a positivist trinity by the *Grand Fétich* (the Earth) and the *Grand Milieu* (Destiny).

The Church of Humanity set up along these lines by Comte's English acolytes soon declined, via the usual schisms and internal wranglings, into a tiny sect of lugubrious fundamentalists. But the informal influence of the cult, with its injunction to 'live for others' ('*vivre pour autrui*', from which we get the word 'altruism'), its practice of meditative reflection on the image and example of an idealised Madonna-figure, and its slightly dispiriting vision of a small sphere of human action encompassed on all sides by the vast indifferent presences of nature and history, percolated deeply into the fibre of late-Victorian middle-class thinking: earnest and glumly improving, prompting Oscar Wilde, the shrewdest as well as the wittiest critic of conventional liberal pieties, to pray for a socialism that, by an equitable distribution of duties and pleasures, would emancipate humankind from 'that sordid necessity of living for others which, in the present condition of things, presses so hardly upon almost everybody' (Wilde 1954: 19). Comte's anti-imperialism, embracing support for the independence of India, Algeria, Brazil and all other colonial dependencies, appealed to socialists and radicals like George Holyoake, one of the founders of the co-operative movement, and E.S. Beesly; and Comtean slogans were adopted by republicans and anti-slavery campaigners in a number of anticolonial revolutions.

His cult of the ideal woman, confined entirely to a domestic and inspirational role, appears again in the figure known, after Coventry Patmore's long sententious poem of that name, as the 'angel in the house', further familiarised for Victorian readers by John Ruskin's essay 'Of Queen's Gardens'. And his hostility towards every variety of supernaturalism and metaphysical idealism helped to propel the popular conception of humanism towards an identification with atheism and secularism that persists to the present day in such essentially nineteenth-century organisations as the Rationalist Press Association, the Ethical Union, and the National Secular Society (Blackham 1976: 129ff.).

Most of all, Comtean ideas inform the work of many of the major novelists of the later nineteenth century, including Emile Zola, George Eliot, George Meredith and Thomas Hardy. Dorothea Brooke, the heroine of Eliot's *Middlemarch* (1871–2), herself, like her author, a Madonna-figure venerated by her admirers, learns in her second marriage (the first having been a disastrous misjudgement) to accept the limitations of the possible, and to resign herself to the sphere of altruistic influence prescribed by a Comtean sexual regime; and the text firmly rebukes any character or reader who may be moved to protest, while omitting to hint that its author, by pursuing a career as a writer and public intellectual and living openly with a married man, had done just that herself:

> No life would have been possible to Dorothea which was not filled with emotion, and she had now a life filled also with a beneficent activity which she had not the doubtful pains of discovering and marking out for herself ... Dorothea could have liked nothing better, since wrongs existed, than that her husband should be in the thick of a struggle against them, and that she should give him wifely help. Many who knew her, thought it a pity that so substantive and rare a creature should have been absorbed into the life of another, and be only known in a certain circle as a wife and mother. But no one stated exactly what else that was in her power she ought rather to have done.
>
> (George Eliot 1965: 894)

Hardy's *The Return of the Native* (1878) opens with a description of a tract of Wessex heathland that might be a concrete metaphor for the indifferent, irreducible materiality of the Comtean universe:

> The untameable, Ishmaelitish thing that Egdon now was it had always been. Civilization was its enemy ... To recline on a stump of thorn in the central valley of Egdon, between afternoon and night, as now, where the eye could reach nothing of the world outside the summits and shoulders of heathland which filled the whole circumference of its glance, and to know that everything around and

underneath had been from prehistoric times as unaltered as the stars overhead, gave ballast to the mind adrift on change.

(Hardy 1995: 33)

and against the background of this 'great inviolable place', Hardy unfolds the story of Clym Yeobright, a young man in whose face 'could be dimly seen the typical countenance of the future' (p. 167). Yeobright's advanced ideas have been fostered by a period of study in Paris, 'where he had become acquainted with ethical systems popular at the time'; his dead mother lives in his memory as 'the sublime saint whose radiance even his tenderness for [his wife] Eustacia could not obscure' (p. 363); and he finds his vocation at last in that most positivist of occupations,

the career of an itinerant open-air preacher and lecturer on morally unimpeachable subjects ... He left alone creeds and systems of philosophy, finding enough and more than enough to occupy his tongue in the opinions and actions common to all good men.

(Hardy 1995: 364–65)

In this sturdily unsentimental English appropriation of Comtean humanism, and in contrast to Feuerbachian idealism, 'Man' figures not as an essential starting-point but as a destination, less a given set of intrinsic qualities than the goal of an epochal and never-to-be-completed process. If there is a 'human condition', it is the condition of being always unconsummated, oscillating ceaselessly between the desire for fulfilment and the consciousness of failure. This is the condition that the nineteenth century called tragic, and identified with modernity. Hardy called it 'the tragedy of unfulfilled aims', and embodied it with searing poignancy in Sue Bridehead and Jude Fawley, the hopeful, questing, doomed protagonists of his most radically searching novel, *Jude the Obscure* (1896); while George Eliot explored it in Maggie Tulliver, the miller's clever daughter in *The Mill on the Floss* (1860), and Tertius Lydgate, the ambitious young physician in *Middlemarch*.

But whether in its tragic or its progressive register, the human predicament figured in nineteenth-century writing is as pervasive and unchanging as the 'eternal note of sadness' that Matthew Arnold heard in the tidal ebb and return of 'Dover Beach':

> Sophocles long ago
> Heard it on the Ægean, and it brought
> Into his mind the turbid ebb and flow
> Of human misery; we
> Find also in the sound a thought,
> Hearing it by this distant northern sea.

The painterly realism of setting and detail, the careful notation of idiom and inflection, serve only to underline the essential timelessness of its enactments. 'It isn't Boston – it's humanity!', retorts the campaigning feminist Olive Chancellor in Henry James' *The Bostonians* (1886) when her southern cousin expresses a wish to visit her home town (James 1966: 20). Humanity, the humanistic 'Man' (always singular, always in the present tense), inhabits not a time or a place but a condition, timeless and unlocalised. This is the burden of Friedrich Nietzsche's radical insight, itself the starting-point for many of the twentieth-century 'antihumanisms' that will be explored in later chapters. 'All philosophers', he wrote in his sardonic critique of contemporary humanism, *Human All Too Human* (1880),

> involuntarily think of 'man' as an *aeterna veritas* [eternal truth], as something that remains constant in the midst of all flux, as a sure measure of things ... Lack of historical sense is the family failing of all philosophers; many, without being aware of it, even take the most recent manifestation of man, such as has arisen under the impress of certain religions, even certain political events, as the fixed form from which one has to start out ... But everything has become: there are no eternal facts, just as there are no absolute truths.
>
> (Hollingdale 1973: 60–61)

'What is needed from now on', he concluded, 'is historical philosophising, and with it the virtue of modesty', the latter a quality with which Nietzsche's name has not often been associated. By modesty he meant a healthy willingness to resist the temptation to confuse our own dispositions and values with some universal and eternal 'human condition'. This he conceived to be one of the four cardinal errors (the others being self-ignorance, the attribution of imaginary qualities to the world around us and 'a false order of rank with animal and nature') which sustain the humanist delusion, and of which he remarked acidly that 'if one deducts the effect of these four errors, one has also deducted away humanity, humaneness and "human dignity"' (Hollingdale 1973: 65).

That remark is a good example of the kind of thing that makes some readers of Nietzsche feel queasy. His sister Elizabeth became in her later years an enthusiastic disciple of the *Führer*, and encouraged the notion that her late brother would have been a keen admirer too. Certainly the Nazis themselves, even then engaged in planning the 'deduction' of humanity on a scale that still beggars imagination, were happy to accept the veneer of intellectual respectability afforded by this association, and misappropriated a number of Nietzschean tropes, such as the *Übermensch* and the 'blond beast', into their own symbolic repertoire. The fact that Martin Heidegger, the most – perhaps the only – serious thinker to commit himself wholeheartedly to Nazism, wrote extensively and approvingly about Nietzsche gave the association a certain credibility. And since it still has some currency, not least in the more intellectual type of neo-Nazi propaganda, it is worth stressing that what is at stake in the Nietzschean critique of the four errors and the 'deduction of humanity' is not the endorsement of genocide but the critical analysis of one of the central myths of nineteenth-century civilisation, its 'religion of humanity', among whose monstrous offspring Nazism itself can be numbered.

2

HUMANISM AND
ANTIHUMANISM

As the archaeology of our thought easily shows, man is an invention
of recent date. And one perhaps nearing its end.

(Michel Foucault)

NIETZSCHE: HUMANISM AS METAPHOR AND
ILLUSION

It would be a mistake to see the relationship between humanism
and antihumanism as one of pure negation or hostility. Not only
do most antihumanisms, as Kate Soper has put it, 'secrete a
humanist rhetoric' (Soper 1986: 182) that betrays their hidden
affinity with what they deny; they generally serve openly humanist ends of intellectual clarity and emancipation, articulated
around a recognisable ethic of human capacity and need.
Nietzsche, the doyen of philosophical antihumanists, was as
surely a product of German humanism as his friend Burckhardt;
and though his membership of the academic establishment,

which he joined in 1869 as a twenty-four-year-old Professor of Classical Philology at the University of Basle, was effectively terminated by the publication three years later of the provocatively unprofessorial *Birth of Tragedy*, his struggle, in the sixteen years that remained before madness closed around him, to formulate a fundamental 'revaluation of all values' returns constantly to humanist themes and figures. Like Burckhardt, he reads the history of modernity as 'the development of the individual', and especially of those exceptional 'complete men' who, confronted with the 'death of God', the absence of any transcendental guarantee of meaning or value, rise above despair to recreate themselves as the bearers of a radical freedom. This heroic transcendence, through the exercise of a 'will to power' that drives every individual to the fullest possible self-realisation, is what Nietzsche calls the *Übermensch* or 'superman'.

At the same time, certain features of his own humanist apprenticeship put Nietzsche in a position to expose the contradictory and (he would have said) fraudulent pretensions of much nineteenth-century humanism. First, as we have seen, the historicism of the classical-Hegelian curriculum alerted him to the provisional and historical character of even the most universalist appeals to an essential humanity. Second, the Lutheran pietism of his upbringing, though soon rejected, left him sharply sensitive to the residual and coercive theology that lurks inside the 'religion of humanity' and other such schemes of secular salvationism, and the tendency of such schemes to conceal quite disreputable motivations beneath their professions of universal altruism: Nietzsche, indeed, rejected the title of philosopher, preferring to style himself an psychologist. Third, and most radical of all, the classicist's habit of looking at propositions philologically (Michel Foucault remarked that all Nietzsche's work was 'no more than the exegesis of a few Greek words') revealed the inescapably figurative nature of all statements:

> What then is truth? A mobile army of metaphors, metonymics, anthropomorphisms – in short, a sum of human relations which, poetically and rhetorically intensified, became transposed and adorned, and which after long usage by a people seem fixed,

> canonical and binding on them. Truths are illusions which one has
> forgotten are illusions, worn-out metaphors which have become
> powerless to affect the sense.
>
> (Nietzsche 1973: 46)

This 'linguistic turn', which Nietzsche called the 'ultimate scepticism', and whose effects can be seen in the 'language games' of the philosopher Ludwig Wittgenstein, the 'discursive formations' anatomised by Foucault and the 'deconstructive' excursions of Jacques Derrida, undermines the credentials of humanism not only in its more inflated or self-serving pretensions but at the very heart. For if the 'humanity' to which it appeals is nothing more than a figure of speech, a metaphor so moribund and inert that we no longer recognise it as such, then what is humanism but a bladder full of hot air?

Nietzsche was not insensitive to the implications of this insight for his own writing. Unlike other philosophers, before and since, he offers his ideas not as truth-statements but as poetic fictions, parables, images, which he makes no attempt to separate from his own mood, temperament and personal circumstances. Indeed, he argued that all statements must be read as metaphors of a particular disposition, physical, psychological, even digestive (he himself was a vegetarian). Distinctions between 'objective' and 'subjective', philosophy and poetry, have no meaning. For the philosopher who wrote that 'I do not know what purely intellectual problems are', and that 'one must want to experience the great problems with one's body and one's soul', the only grounds that remain for distinguishing between statements are the force, authenticity and passion with which they are uttered: their 'will to power'.

Clearly, this could be (and has been) used to license a good deal of unscrupulous lying, bullying and, harnessed to an anti-Semitic nationalism that Nietzsche himself abominated, much worse. But such risks, for a philosopher whose motto was 'live dangerously', were unavoidable. While Comte tried to cobble up a makeshift quasi-religion on the site and the sentiments vacated by the collapse of Christianity, Nietzsche's intuition was more radical, and more disturbing: that for a civilisation so saturated in Judaeo-Christian beliefs and values that even its atheisms sound like liturgical pieties, the 'death of God' signals not only the end of theology but the demise of truth in all its forms, the unravelling of meaning itself. In those circumstances, bereft of authority and faced with nihilistic despair, there is nothing to do but start from scratch with what remains: a rebellious bundle of bodily and psychic needs, a deep urge to survive and transcend, a treacherous and indispensable language.

Nietzsche apart, some of the most searching criticism of the positivist 'religion of humanity' came from the philosopher and political economist John Stuart Mill. Mill admired Comte, acknowledging that with all its pompous absurdities the cult of the Great Being was an attempt to appease a genuine hunger for meaning, to replenish the ideological vacancy that had been created by the feebleness and irrelevance of the Church in the face of capitalist civilisation. The objection to Comte, Mill argued, lay not in the notion of a secular religion itself but in the ruthlessness with which he subordinated the variety of human interest and need to a single programme. The *System of Positive Politics*, he argued, portended 'a despotism of society over the individual, surpassing anything contemplated in the political ideal of the most rigid disciplinarian among the ancient philosophers' (Mill 1969: 338). Anticipating many a later confrontation between English pragmatism and Gallic 'theory', he found the root of the problem

in an original mental twist, very common in French thinkers, and by which M. Comte was distinguished beyond them all. He could not dispense with what he called 'unity'. The *fons errorum* [source of error] in M. Comte's later speculations is this inordinate demand for 'unity' and 'systematization' ... Why is it necessary that all human life should point but to one object, and be cultivated into a system of means to a single end?

(Mill 1969: 336)

Mill was the son of a prominent utilitarian, a friend and colleague of the Great Cham of utilitarianism, Jeremy Bentham, who argued that the rightness or wrongness of an action should be judged solely in terms of its utility (defined as its capacity to produce or increase pleasure), and that the aim of a civilised society must be to ensure 'the greatest happiness of the greatest number', an outcome that can be measured with mathematical precision. Mill's recoil from the emotional aridity of these ideas is vividly recounted in his autobiography, in which he recalls the life-changing experience, after years of enduring James Mill's unrelentingly cerebral regime of domestic instruction that began with Greek at the age of three, of discovering the early visionary poetry of Wordsworth (see Mill 1873, chapter 3). But the younger Mill retained much of the utilitarian programme, including its oddly joyless computations of happiness (the 'felicific calculus') and the radical individualism that Bentham shared with contemporaries like Thomas Paine and William Blake. 'May it not be the fact', he asked,

> that mankind, who after all are made up of single human beings, obtain a greater sum of happiness when each pursues his own, under the rules and conditions required by the greater good of the rest?
> (Mill 1969: 336–37)

Comte, in contrast, thinks of humanity as an undifferentiated mass, waiting to be bullied and cajoled by the enlightened few into a programmed uniformity of spiritual felicity.

> Liberty and spontaneity on the part of individuals form no part of the scheme ... Every particular of conduct, public or private, is to be open to the public eye, and to be kept, by the power of opinion, in the course which the spiritual corporation shall judge to be the most right.
> (Mill 1969: 327)

Eighty years later, in the shadow of the Second World War, this verdict was to be endorsed in more brutal terms by Jean-Paul Sartre:

> The cult of humanity ends in Comtian humanism, shut-in upon itself, and – this must be said – in Fascism.
> (Sartre 1948: 32)

Liberty and spontaneity: the coupling of the two themes discloses the ideological lineage, with all its ambiguities, of the liberal humanism of which Mill, the political economist whose writings *On Liberty* (1859) and *The Subjection of Women* (1869) enjoy classic status in the liberal canon, is a founding figure. 'Liberty' recalls the Miltonic and Rousseauist complexion of radical enlightenment, with its discourse of individual rights and freedoms, guaranteed by reason and natural law; while 'spontaneity' evokes the sister-tradition, 'romantic' and anti-rationalist, of Wordsworthian feeling. Marx called this interweaving of romantic and utilitarian strains in Victorian liberalism a 'legitimate antithesis', meaning that there was no genuine contradiction between the two, merely an alternation of moods in the bourgeois disposition (Marx 1973a: 162). In the sense that the romantic revolt against the chilly despotism of enlightened reason, Keats's call for 'a life of sensations rather than a life of thoughts', is a revolt in gesture only, he was of course right. We might add, too, that in tempering the 'masculine' discipline of rational freedom with the 'feminine' attractions of imaginative spontaneity, liberal humanism served both to obscure and to legitimise the real contradictions of capitalist and patriarchal 'liberty'.

But the antithesis can still generate its own force and drama, especially when, as in the confrontation in Charles Dickens' *Hard Times* (1854) between the chilly pragmatism of the utilitarian Thomas Gradgrind, 'a man of facts and calculations ... with a rule and a pair of scales, and the multiplication table always in his pocket, sir, ready to weigh and measure any parcel of human nature, and tell you exactly what it comes to', and the disreputable human warmth of Sleary the circus-master, its tensions are fully exposed; and it has proved a remarkably durable constant in English cultural and political life over the last hundred years. Prose and poetry, reason and emotion, hard fact and imaginative value, the 'two cultures' of technology and art: the oppositions engage and disengage compulsively, marking out the resilient strengths of the 'English ideology' as well as its disabling limitations.

LIBERAL HUMANISM

'The Utilitarian social philosophy of Jeremy Bentham,' writes a historian of humanism, leavened and made wholesome by John Stuart Mill's postscript *On Liberty*, translated into a modern idiom and brought up to date with new possibilities, new necessities and new dangers, is the humanist social philosophy today, and substantially will be permanently so.

(Blackham 1976: 55)

But this complacent assurance of continuity and permanence, though dispiritingly typical of much official humanism today, fails to register the growing desperation of the humanist project in the decades either side of the First World War. After Mill, perhaps the most talismanic figure for an increasingly troubled and sceptical liberal humanism is the novelist and essayist E.M. Forster, many of whose formulations of its central dilemmas have acquired a proverbial currency. His hope that, faced with the choice of betraying a friend or betraying his country, 'I should have the guts to betray my country', like his decision to offer no more than 'two cheers for Democracy' on the grounds that 'only Love, the Beloved Republic' deserves three, expresses the categorical priority of concrete individuals over abstract systems, of the private over the public, while regretfully acknowledging the inescapable claims of the latter (Forster 1965: 76, 78); and the defining antithesis itself is expressed in his famous injunction to 'connect the prose and the passion ... Live in fragments no longer, only connect' (Forster 1941: 174–75).

This is the characteristic timbre of English liberal humanism: small-scale, individualist, suspicious of big theories and sweeping solutions. Forster's affinities as a novelist are with the understated ironies and obliquities of Jane Austen rather than the Comtean homiletics of George Eliot; and as a thinker, his 'law-givers', he wrote in 1939, 'are Erasmus and Montaigne, not Moses and St Paul' (1965: 75), an antithesis which might have puzzled the Christian humanists of the sixteenth century, but which signals a preference for the dialogical and ironic over the solemnly monological, for scepticism over belief, questions over answers. The modest affiliations of friendship and the claims of personal loyalty take precedence always over the regimented compulsions of system, movement or cause.

The phrase 'only connect' supplies the leitmotif for Forster's 'condition of England' novel *Howards End* (1910), whose plot reads like an allegory of the troubled polarities of liberal humanism in the years before the Great War. Margaret Schlegel, musical, cultured, Anglo-German, whose very name associates her allusively with the philosopher Friedrich Schlegel, one of the pivotal figures of romantic *Humanismus*, inherits the country house of the title from a friend, then restores it to its original ownership by marrying the friend's widowed husband, the prosaic businessman Henry Wilcox. The connection seems complete, the antitheses of industry and culture, prose and passion, satisfyingly resolved. But not entirely. As one chapter reminds us, with a sardonic acknowledgement that a novel of this kind, minutely attentive to the finely tuned sensibilities of the cultivated and the well-to-do, cannot transcend the ideology that constitutes it: 'We are not concerned with the very poor. They are unthinkable' (Forster 1941: 44). The circles of civilised 'connection' are sympathetically but firmly closed to the plebeian, the philistine, the too earnestly aspiring. But the home-counties idyll of the Schlegels and Wilcoxes is irreparably disrupted nonetheless by the plaintive presence and violent death of the suburban bank clerk Leonard Bast, lower middle class and pathetically hungry for 'culture', whose posthumous child Margaret's sister is carrying as the novel moves to its uneasy ending.

If the closure of *Howards End* seems troubled and irresolute, the final pages of Forster's next novel, *A Passage to India* (1924), feel more like deadlock. In the last of the novel's three 'movements', the young Muslim physician Aziz, acquitted in a dramatic court case of sexual assault on an Englishwoman, but deeply embittered by the experience and now active in the independence movement, meets an old friend, the liberal-minded English schoolteacher Fielding, and they go riding together. 'Why', asks the Englishman, invoking the deepest touchstone of Forsterian humanism, 'can't we be friends now?' But at that moment

> they swerved apart; the earth didn't want it, sending up rocks through which the riders must pass single file; the temples, the tank, the jail, the palace, the birds, the carrion, the Guest House, that

came into view as they issued from the gap and saw Mau beneath; they didn't want it, they said in their hundred voices, 'No, not yet,' and the sky said, 'No, not there'.

(Forster 1961: 317)

The novel, and Forster's career as a novelist, come to a halt there, half-hopeful, half-despairing, suspended in a limbo of baffled disconnection. Fielding mocks the 'abstract hate' of his friend's independence rhetoric ('India shall be a nation! No foreigners of any sort! ... Hurrah for India!'), and the text acknowledges the mockery as just, but the idea that friendship between English-man and Indian can heal centuries of systematic prejudice and exploitation is revealed as no less absurd, a notion at once evasive and condescending.

The critic F.R. Leavis called *A Passage to India* 'a classic of the liberal spirit' (Leavis 1962: 277), but it is just as surely one of its limit-texts, exposing the impotence of humanist decency in the face of racism, and its unhappy but inescapable complicity with the realities of imperial rule. The genre of the novel, at least of the kind of novel to which Forster remained ruefully faithful, rooted as it is in the primacy of relationships between rational individuals and essentially comic in spirit even when tragic in circumstance, is the liberal-humanist form *par excellence*, and Forster's decision to abandon it after the impasse of his Indian story says something of wider significance about the demoralisa-tion of liberal opinion in the grim decades between the two world wars, and something too about its incapacity. In an essay on 'Jew-consciousness' published in 1939, Forster deplored the resurgence of anti-Semitic prejudice and advised his readers that 'for the moment, all that we can do is to dig in our heels, and prevent silliness from sliding into insanity' (1965: 26). Judge-ment is never easy, in the thick of things, and hindsight is the cheapest of complacencies; but to think of anti-Semitism, then, only weeks before the German invasion of Poland, as a 'silliness' that can still be prevented by sensible people digging in their heels betrays the limitations of an individualistic humanism that sees only trees, not forests, and sees them from the standpoint of a cultivated English leisure-class intellectual, a latter-day Tom

Brown for whom 'if the average man is anyone in particular he is a preparatory school boy' (ibid.: 24).

It is instructive to compare Forster with another novelist and humanist, his German contemporary Thomas Mann. Mann shared Forster's commitment to the irrevocable priority of the rational and human, along with his distaste for the regimental vulgarities of mass politics and ideology. In 1918, amid the wreckage of the First World War, he had contended that the blame for the war must be attributed to the hijacking by political demagogues of the concept of 'humanity',

> this favourite word of rhetorical democracy, which has been anointed with all the oils of French rhetoric and Anglo-Saxon cant,

and argued that an authentic humanism could have no commerce with politics of any kind:

> it has never seemed possible to me that anyone could disagree that 'humanity', a human way of thinking and observing, obviously signifies the opposite of all politics. To think and to reflect in a human way means to think and to reflect in a nonpolitical way.
>
> (Mann 1983: 315)

But by the later 1930s, while Forster was scolding Nazism for its schoolboy 'silliness', Mann had concluded that it was precisely the fastidious political abstinence of liberal bourgeois like himself that had permitted it to happen, and that he could not absolve his class and his generation of responsibility for the approaching catastrophe.

That realisation is the subject of Mann's most searching exploration of the relations between humanist and Nazi rationalities, the novel *Doctor Faustus* (1947). The decision to rework the Faust story has a special resonance, for the semi-legendary figure of Georg (in some versions Johann) Faust or (the Latinised form) Faustus of Wittenberg, magus and diabolist, haunts the German imagination, articulating its deepest anxieties at critical moments of change and confrontation. The revolutionary antinomies of rational enlightenment and romantic transcendence find their ¹efinitive expression in Goethe's dramatic poem *Faust*. Nietzsche, developing Heine's theme, characterised the German temperament as an antithesis of philistine and Faustian qualities. For the Munich *Gymnasium* teacher Oswald Spengler, chronicler of *The Decline of the West*, the Faustian signified not only Germany but European *Humanismus* as a whole, then (in 1918) about to enter its final twilight. But strictly Teutonic associations of *Volk* and *Geist* dominate later readings of the figure, increasingly so as German nationalism approaches its demonic pact with fascism. Herman Amonn (*Dämon Faust*, 1932) found in Goethe's poem an allegory of 'the development of the Faustian, that is of German culture'; while Alfred Rosenberg, ideologue of early Nazism and purveyor of the anti-Semitic imposture called the 'Protocols of the Elders of Zion' (1923), wrote in *The Myth of the Twentieth Century* (1930) that 'Goethe presents in *Faust* our undying *essence*, which lies behind every outpouring of our spirit in its new guise' (Smeed 1975: 29–30).

This is the background to Mann's story of the composer Adrian Leverkühn, whose innovative genius is the reward for a Faustian bargain that plunges him finally into madness and death even as Germany itself rushes towards self-immolation around him. The story is told by Leverkühn's childhood friend Serenus Zeitblom, professor of Classics and humanist, who represents with comic pomposity the values of enlightened *Bildung* ('Here, as so often,' he muses contentedly, 'I cannot help dwelling on the inward, the almost mysterious connexion of the old philological interest with a lively and loving sense of the beauty and dignity of reason in the human being' (Mann 1968: 14)), and whose appalled observation of his friend's imaginative derangement forces him to confront the intolerable coupling of the rational and the demonic, Nietzsche's Apollo and Dionysus, within the genius of European civilisation itself.

Early in the novel the philhellenic Zeitblom recalls a youthful visit to Athens, during which, standing upon the Acropolis, and looking down on the Sacred Way along which the initiates had once made their way to Eleusis to celebrate the ritual mysteries of the goddess Demeter, he

> experienced by divination the rich feeling of life which expressed itself in the initiate veneration of Olympic Greece for the deities of

the depths; often, later on, I explained to my pupils that culture is in
very truth the pious and regulating, I might say propitiatory, entrance
of the dark and uncanny into the service of the gods.

(Mann 1968: 15)

But nothing in his complacent academicism can prepare him for
the true horror of the dark and uncanny, as it erupts in his friend
and his country, and about which there is nothing remotely
'pious and regulating'. The desolating 'panic and emptiness' that
lie always in ambush for Forster's hopes of human connection
assume in Mann's novel the concrete form of the hero's syphilitic
dementia and his country's 'monstrous national perversion', and
Zeitblom's plaintive questions,

Shall I once more impress upon the hearts of my top-form pupils in
the humanities the cultural ideas in which reverence for the deities of
the depths blends with the civilized cult of Olympian reason and
clarity? ... Must I not ask myself whether or not I did right?

(Mann 1968: 485)

fall unanswered into an abyss of futility and self-reproach.

Forster and Mann have much in common. Both represent, with
clarity and candour, the virtues, and the final insufficiency, of the
heritage of nineteenth-century liberal humanism. For both, as it
happens, those virtues, rationality, belief in human progress,
courageous individuality, were embodied most fully not in literature but in music, above all in the music of Beethoven, the
composer who more than any other incarnates the values and
contradictions of enlightened and romantic *Humanismus*. In
Howards End, the Fifth Symphony conjures the spectral goblins
of panic and emptiness only to cast them out in the last movement in a Promethean affirmation of reason and order (Forster
1941: 33); and in *Doctor Faustus* another great work in C minor
and major, the last piano sonata opus 111, is offered as the
touchstone of demonic energy and terror harnessed to rational
sympathy and control (Mann 1968: 55–57). Both wrote through
and about the last days of empires. Both recognised, as others
less honest or perceptive have failed to do, that the humanist and

the imperialist share a common patrimony, and that amid the débâcle of empire humanism too must be called to account.

MODERNISM AND ANTIHUMANISM

The major challenge, when it comes, is philosophical and ideological, and issues from the continental heartland of philosophical humanism itself: Heidegger, Adorno, Althusser, Foucault. But a critique of humanism has already played an important part in the theoretical formulation of literary modernism in the earlier part of the century. Rejecting what T.E. Hulme called the 'slop and romanticism' of an art expressive of human experience and aspiration, Anglo-American modernists called for an aesthetic of 'geometric' impersonality (Hulme 1924: 77). W.B. Yeats abandoned romantic nationalism ('all that is personal soon rots') in favour of a poetry 'cold and passionate as the dawn'; 'You mustn't look in my novel for the old stable Ego of the character', advised D.H. Lawrence, and T.S. Eliot insisted that 'poetry is not the expression of personality, but an escape from personality', that there should be the greatest possible distance between 'the man who suffers and the mind which creates' (Yeats 1961: 69; Lawrence 1981: 183; T.S. Eliot 1920: 54, 58). Antihumanism, we remember, frequently 'secretes a humanist rhetoric' (Soper 1986: 128), and it is true that Eliot's antithesis of suffering 'man' (as ever) and creative 'mind' merely reformulates the Kantian distinction between the 'phenomenal' world and our 'noumenal' knowledge of it. But the impulse behind literary modernism betrays an authentic antihumanism, indeed a revulsion against the human; 'a desire for austerity and bareness', Hulme called it, 'a striving towards structure and away from the messiness and confusion of nature and natural things' (1924: 96). In his hatred of romantic and liberal-humanist 'slop', Hulme outdistanced even Nietzsche, whom he loftily associated with a Burkhardtian nostalgia for the Renaissance:

> There are people who, disgusted with romanticism, wish for us to go back to the classical period, or who, like Nietzsche, wish us to

admire the Renaissance. But such partial reactions will always fail, for they are only half measures – it is no good returning to humanism, for that will itself degenerate into romanticism.

(Hulme 1924: 62)

Against this, he advocated the 'religious attitude', itself not easily distinguishable, for all its air of ultra-modernity, from a regressive turn to the pre-humanist 'middle ages', the 'austerity and bareness' of the monastic life, the security and 'structural' impersonality of an infallible Church. 'Dante and Shakespeare divide the modern world between them,' wrote Eliot; 'there is no third (Eliot 1951). Dante, unrelenting laureate, for Eliot at least, of doctrinal orthodoxy, confronts Shakespeare, supreme chronicler of the human in all its 'messiness and confusion', and the confrontation does not permit compromise.

I have called this modernist antihumanism 'aesthetic', but of course it is political too. 'Before Copernicus', Hulme told an audience in 1914, deftly hijacking Burckhardt's narrative of heroic individualism only to explode it,

man was not the centre of the world; after Copernicus he was. You get a change from a certain profundity and intensity to that flat and insipid optimism which, passing through its first stage of decay in Rousseau, has finally culminated in the state of slush in which we have the misfortune to live ... the re-emergence of geometrical art may be the precursor of the re-emergence of the corresponding attitude towards the world, and so, of the break up of the Renaissance humanistic attitude.

(Hulme 1924: 80)

The search for a lost profundity and intensity led Hulme, as it was to lead Eliot, to an admiration for the Catholic and royalist authoritarianism of Charles Maurras' proto-fascist *Action Française*. The same impulse turned Ezra Pound into an eccentric but energetically committed apologist for full-blown fascism. In Pound's case it also inspired one of the more baroque conspiracy theories of modern times, in which the filthy 'slop' and 'slush' of humanist sentimentality ('an old bitch gone in the teeth') was identified with the double menace threatening the renewal of Aryan civilisation: women and Jews. Abandoning his earlier hope of 'driving any new idea into the great passive vulva of London', he retired to fascist Pisa, where the hysterical machismo and xenophobia of Mussolini's bombast provided a more congenial context for his musings on the twin evils of contraception and usury, and the danger they posed for that 'great clot of seminal fluid', the (male) artist's brain.

The question 'Who is man?', Martin Heidegger told students of his Nietzsche seminar at the University of Freiburg in the soon-to-be-interrupted summer semester of 1939, 'is not as harmless as it might seem'.

> This question is to be Europe's task for the future, for this century and the century to come. It can find its answer only in the exemplary and authoritative way in which particular nations, in competition with others, shape their history.
>
> (Heidegger 1984: 102)

Like many others in that fateful summer, Heidegger was well aware that the impending contest of nations would be of a scale and consequence unparalleled in the history of conflict. He saw it, indeed, as the transition from 'the preparatory phase of the modern age – the time between 1600 and 1900 – to the beginning of its consummation', a process whose outcome could not be guaranteed.

> We do not know the time-span of this consummation. Presumably, it will either be very brief and catastrophic or else very long, in the sense of a self-perpetuating arrangement of what has been attained. There is no room for halfway measures in the present stage of the history of our planet ... at some point and in some way the historical decision arises as to whether this final age is the conclusion of Western history or the counterpart of another beginning.
>
> (Heidegger 1987: 6, 8)

Few of those who survived it are likely to have looked back on the period that began with the German invasion of Czechoslovakia in March 1939, and ended with the atomic devastation of Hiroshima and Nagasaki and the Japanese surrender in August 1945, as a second Renaissance. For many, it looked more like the end not of an era, but of a world: the death of an idea, a terminus of the humanly conceivable. Who, faced with the reality of those years, could still retrieve anything usable in the idea of the human: the global scale and indiscriminate totality of the slaughter, the contemptuous brutality and humiliation inflicted on prisoners, partisans and resident populations in Burma, Central Europe and the Balkans, above all the realisation, as the camps were opened and the films, the photographs, the meticulous documentation unearthed, of the unfathomable cold horror of the *Endlösung*, the 'final solution' to the 'racial problem'? The very word, like the apocalyptic *Götterdämmerung* fantasies of the Nazi intellectuals who coined it, suggests a sinister terminality. But for all the Wagnerian and gothic primitivism in which the Third Reich chose to project its public personality, there was no escaping the recognition that the systematic purging of Jews, homosexuals and other racial impurities was the result not of some inexplicable descent into irrational, atavistic barbarity but of a supremely modern rationality. The cool framing of objectives, the logical planning of complex systems, the orderly deployment of technology and resources: all these testify to a piece of demographic engineering as measured in its symmetry, as eloquent in its appalling fashion of individual genius and collective enterprise as the Parthenon itself.

In the face of this, it seemed, not only humanism, the rational self-assertive world-changing humanism of the Greeks, the Renaissance and the Enlightenment, but the very notion of the *human* was called to account. Confronted with the death-camps, George Steiner has argued, language itself falls silent. Theodor Adorno, for whom they only made explicit the ruthless will to power that had always been implicit in the project of rational 'enlightenment', believed that they had cancelled the possibility of poetry, the unconstrained voice of humanist individuality. For the camp commanders, like their masters in Berlin, were lovers of poetry, not brutes; and language itself, Hamlet's 'discourse of reason', could not be acquitted of complicity in their monstrous undertaking (Steiner 1969: 76; Adorno 1973: 3). For the post-war generations, what has come to be known as the *Shoah* or Holocaust represents the vanishing point, the absolute zero of what is thinkable. In spite of the vast amount that has been written and said about it, the novels and memoirs, the sober academic treatises and the impassioned denunciations, the films, the justifications, even the denials that it ever happened at all, it presents what philosophers call an *aporia*, a maze or wilderness of thought from which no exit can be found; or, perhaps, one of those tests which it is fatal to fail, and even more catastrophic to pass, like the Theban Sphinx's riddling question to the young Oedipus, the answer to which, according to the legend, was 'Man'.

THE TWILIGHT OF LIBERAL HUMANISM

Their eternal position in the divine order is something of which we are only conscious as a setting whose irrevocability can but serve to heighten the effect of their humanity, preserved for us in all its force. The result is a direct experience of life which overwhelms everything else, a comprehension of human realities which spreads as widely and variously as it goes to the very roots of our emotions, an illumination of man's impulses and passions which leads us to share in them without restraint and indeed to admire their variety and their greatness. And by virtue of this immediate and admiring sympathy with man, the principle, rooted in the divine order, of the indestructibility of the whole historical and individual man turns against that order, makes it subservient to its own purposes, and obscures it. The image of man eclipses the image of God ... More accurately than antique literature was ever able to present it, we are given to see, in the realm of timeless being, the history of man's inner life and unfolding.

(Auerbach 1968: 201–2)

That description of the characters in Dante's *Divine Comedy* was written, some time between May 1942 and April 1945, in Istanbul, where its author, the German scholar Erich Auerbach, was teaching at the Turkish State University. At first sight, the passage stands in unbroken continuity with Burckhardt, for whom the Florentine poet bestrides 'the boundary between medievalism and modern times', and who wrote that in his work 'the human spirit had taken a mighty step toward the consciousness of its own secret life' (Burckhardt 1958: 308). Like Arnold's Chaucer, Auerbach's Dante is the great proto-humanist, the first medieval writer to break out of the constraints of a theology in which human beings figure only as illustrative evidence of the power of an omnipotent deity (the ostensible structure of the poem) and to present them as independent beings, in all the three-dimensional variety of their historical and psychological individuality.

The subtitle of Auerbach's *Mimesis*, from which the passage is taken, is 'the representation of reality in Western literature', and specifically the development and eventual breakdown and transformation of what we now call 'realism'. But interwoven with that theme is another: the emergence of the 'human' as the central topic of European literature, a figure now also facing a possible dissolution. Starting (where else?) with Homer, the book traces a line that runs through Late Roman and medieval writing to humanists like Rabelais, Montaigne and Cervantes, and the fully developed realism of the eighteenth and nineteenth-century novel, and comes to rest at last in the post-realist fiction of Virginia Woolf, in whose dissolving and intermingling subjectivities Auerbach discerns the appearance of a new humanity, embodied not in the heroic individuals of epic, romance and realist narrative but in the anonymous ordinariness of common life:

> To be sure, what happens in that moment – be it outer or inner processes – concerns in a very personal way the individuals who live in it, but it also (and for that very reason) concerns the elementary things which men in general have in common ... The more numerous, varied, and simple the people are who appear as subjects of such random moments, the more effectively must what they have in common shine forth.
>
> (Auerbach 1968: 552)

Furthermore, Woolf's 'unprejudiced and exploratory type of representation' must be seen as evidence of a change in the general conditions of life as momentous as that to which Dante in his time was witness, for in it 'we cannot but see to what an extent – below the surface conflicts – the differences between men's ways of life and forms of thought have already lessened' (ibid.: 552).

The 'surface conflicts' were hardly negligible. A contemplative eye might appreciate the poignant historical symmetry that led the last of the German humanists to write his history of European literature in the very city from which the Byzantine Greek Chrysoloras had set out five and a half centuries before to instruct Dante's compatriots in the language of Homer. But for Auerbach, ousted by the Nazis from the chair of romance philology at the University of Marburg, the journey to neutral Istanbul was an act not of pilgrimage but of enforced exile. In beleaguered wartime Turkey, books were scarce; written without the help of the scholarly libraries which western intellectuals have learnt to take for granted, *Mimesis* is above all an astonishing feat of recollection, the reconstruction of a two-thousand-year tradition at the very moment in which it is about to pass into memory.

It is also, unmistakably, an obituary. Though the 'common life of mankind on earth' which he detects in Woolf's mingling streams of consciousness is welcomed (for there is none of his countryman Adorno's aristocratic distaste for the 'massification of culture'), it is with regret and a certain foreboding:

> the complicated process of dissolution which led to the fragmentation of the exterior action, to reflection of consciousness, and to stratification of time seems to be tending toward a very simple solution. Perhaps it will be too simple to please those who, despite all its dangers and catastrophes, admire and love our epoch for the sake of its abundance of life and the incomparable historical vantage point which it affords. But they are few in number, and probably they will not live to see much more than the first forewarnings of the approaching unification and simplification.
>
> (ibid.: 552–53)

For Auerbach, no less than for Forster, the realism of the great European novelists from Cervantes to Proust is the child of liberal humanism, and of the intellectual culture, leisured, bourgeois and 'western', that nurtured it. Both went on writing and lecturing for several years after the war, Forster in Cambridge and Auerbach in Princeton; but both recognised that their era was over, and acknowledged that recognition in the concluding 'not yet ... not there' of their finest work. In one of the most revealing chapters in *Mimesis*, Auerbach speculates on the implications of Goethe's distaste for the revolutionary movements of his time, his unwillingness to relate the personal lives and intellectual interests of his characters to the public events and historical processes by which they were shaped. Goethe, he notes, 'never represented the reality of contemporary social life dynamically, as the germ of developments in process and in the future'. Instead, when compelled to comment on public life, 'he does so in general reflections, and these are almost always value judgements: they are predominantly mistrustful and disapproving'. The relevance of this to Auerbach's contemporaries is unmistakable. Like Eliot and Leavis (on the 'right') or the 'Frankfurt School' of Adorno and Marcuse (on the 'left'), Goethe reserved a particular disapproval for the 'technical development of machinery' and 'the progressively conscious participation of the masses in public life', from which, like them, he feared 'a shallowing of intellectual life', with 'nothing to make up for such a loss' (Auerbach 1968: 451).

How precisely these anxieties foreshadow the debates about mechanisation and mass society in the twentieth century, debates which, in spite of a dashing 'postmodern' respray in recent years, have scarcely moved on since the 1950s, needs no emphasis (see Swingewood 1977). With rare exceptions, the reaction of humanist intellectuals to the industrialisation of social and cultural life and the emergence of mass politics has been one of patrician disdain or nauseated revulsion. But how differently things might have turned out, Auerbach muses, if Goethe, the prototype of Mann's 'unpolitical man', had been willing to engage himself with the popular movements which, in different circumstances, might have unified Germany in his lifetime.

> If that had happened then, perhaps too the integration of Germany into the emerging new reality of Europe and the world might have been prepared more calmly, have been accomplished with fewer

uncertainties and less violence ... as we look back upon all that has
happened since, we are tempted to imagine what effect might have
been exerted upon German literature and German society, if Goethe,
with his vigorous sensuality, his mastery of life, his far-reaching and
untrammeled vision, had devoted more interest and constructive
effort to the emerging modern structure of life.

(Auerbach 1968: 451–52)

The figure that broods over this poignant reverie, written, probably, as the cities of Germany were engulfed in fire and Hitler's
war-machine plunged towards its Faustian catastrophe, is of
course the humanist paradigm: the Platonic philosopher-king,
Machiavelli's Prince, Nietzsche's *Übermensch*. At the end, as at the
beginning, the solitary thinker dreams, redrawing the world in
the imagined symmetries of knowledge and power.

SOCIALIST HUMANISM AND THEORETICAL ANTIHUMANISM

In the summer of 1964 a little-known French Communist academic called Louis Althusser published in an obscure Communist Party journal an article on the subject of 'Marxism and
Humanism', reprinted a couple of years later in a collection of
essays *Pour Marx*, and translated into English in 1969 as *For
Marx*. To anyone not professionally involved in the theoretical
and political contentions of that excitable period, the influence
and prestige of this highly technical and rather arid ten-page essay,
and the heat it was able to generate, must seem astonishing. The
most spectacular, if belated, response, for English-speaking readers, was the violent assault on Althusser, at times pungently
witty and angry, but all too often tiresomely prolix and self-
indulgent, in E.P. Thompson's *The Poverty of Theory* (1978). But
for every reader provoked to Thompsonian indignation by the
essay's coldly contemptuous dismissal of every variety of humanism, there were many who happily embraced its determination to
fumigate the 'scientific' certainties of Marxism against the sentimental
delusions of 'ideological' humanism. More than any other text, it
was responsible for establishing the formidable credentials of

'theoretical anti-humanism', and for turning 'humanism' itself, for a couple of decades at least, into a term of sovereign condemnation.

Althusser roots his argument, which is an assault not only on humanism in general but particularly on Marxist or socialist humanism, in the writings of 'the Old Man', Marx himself. Early on in his career, he argues, the young Marx, in a decisive theoretical *'coupure'* or break, parted company with the humanistic premises and pieties of the philosophical tradition on which he himself had been nurtured, the idealistic tradition of Kant, Hegel and Feuerbach, and formulated a model of history and society based not on humanistic notions of will, freedom or human potential but on such 'structural' concepts as class, ideology and the forces and relations of production. 'In 1845', we are told,

> Marx broke radically with every theory that based history and politics on an essence of man ... This rupture with every *philosophical* anthropology or humanism is no secondary detail; it is Marx's scientific discovery ... The earlier idealist ('bourgeois') philosophy depended in all its domains and arguments (its 'theory of knowledge', its conception of history, its political economy, its ethics, its aesthetics, etc.) on a problematic of *human nature* (or the essence of man) ... By rejecting the essence of man as his theoretical basis, Marx rejected the whole of this organic system of postulates.
>
> (Althusser 1969: 227)

The 'break' identified by Althusser in Marx's early writings, and fiercely disputed by his critics, is, he insists, theoretical and philosophical, not ethical or practical. It is perfectly consistent for a 'theoretical antihumanist' to be a practical 'humanist': to be fond of children, subscribe to Oxfam and Amnesty and help old ladies across the road. Indeed, he argues, a certain pragmatic humanism of rights and freedoms, however ideological and theoretically unsound, may be a necessary fiction in the mucky business of political organisation and struggle. Attempts by some of his opponents to represent him as a monster, a view that did not scruple to draw support from his tragic killing of his wife during a period of depressive insanity, or a covert apologist for Stalinist tyranny (Edward Thompson's position) are wide of the mark. At the same time, the tidy distinction he draws between the clinical procedures of Marxist 'science' ('theoretical practice') and the fumbling misconceptions of ideology, a surprisingly 'Cartesian' distinction for a philosopher who rejected Descartes' humanistic idealism and empiricism, invites misreading, and can too easily imply an insulting condescension towards all those movements for national, sexual, cultural or intellectual emancipation that continue to draw their energy and define their ends from humanist ideas of liberty and self-realisation.

This presumption arises in part from too pre-emptive and simplified a notion of the 'humanist subject', the ideal 'piece of work' (*Hamlet*, II, ii, 98) or paradigmatic 'man' who is enthroned at the heart of all the discourses of humanism. Of course, as Marx famously argued, the most powerful ideas in any epoch are the ideas of the powerful, and it requires no particular ingenuity to demonstrate that the essential human being tends in any period to bear a striking resemblance to the dominant group of that time and place. Michèle Barrett puts this engagingly:

> Let us imagine the celebrated 'Cartesian subject'. He is made in the image of his inventor. He is white, a European; he is highly educated, he thinks and is sensitive, he can probably even think in Latin and Greek; he lived a bit too soon to be a bourgeois, but he has class confidence; he has a general confidence in his existence and power; he is not a woman, not black, not a migrant, not marginal; he is heterosexual and a father ... It is entirely clear to us that this model of the subject is centred, and unified, around a nexus of social and biographical characteristics that represent power.
>
> (Barrett 1991: 90)

But, as Barrett argues, this parodic mannequin and his later equivalents are much more contradictory and unstable figures than the Althusserian critique of the 'humanist subject' supposes; and in any case, it is stupid and unnecessary to conclude that because they have so often secreted the lineaments and interests of a powerful minority within a generalising rhetoric of universal humanity, humanity itself is a hopelessly contaminated concept, to be thrown out with the dirty bathwater of humanist delusion.

Rejecting the historicism and humanism that imagine 'man' bestriding a history of his own making and directing it to his own ends, in favour of a theory of structural positions, causations and transformations, Althusser's Marxism has been called 'structuralist', and its premisses located, like those of other structuralists such as the psychoanalyst Jacques Lacan and the anthropologist Claude Lévi-Strauss, in the psychological writings of Freud and the structural linguistics of Ferdinand de Saussure. Freud saw himself as an *Aufklärer*, a humanistic rationalist of the old school, dispelling error and superstition and throwing the murkiest corners of the psyche open to the sunlight of scientific reason. But his demonstration of the fragility of conscious selfhood, its enslavement to irrational drives and unformulated wishes over which it has little control, removed the philosophical supports of enlightened rationality and punctured its illusions of sovereignty. And just as psychoanalysis dethroned 'man' from the control of his own mental life, so Saussurean linguistics cashiered him from command over his own speech, by showing that the sovereign 'discourse of reason', the singular utterance ('Speak, that I may see thee' (Jonson 1975: 435)), is no more than a local manifestation of the great system of language itself, to whose metropolitan and impersonal laws it is wholly subordinate.

In this manoeuvre, structuralism kicks away the twin pillars of humanism: the sovereignty of rational consciousness, and the authenticity of individual speech. I do not think, I am thought. You do not speak, you are spoken. Thought and speech, which for the humanist had been the central substance of identity, are located elsewhere, and the self is a vacancy. 'I', as Althusser's compatriot the poet Arthur Rimbaud put it almost a century earlier, 'is Another' (Rimbaud 1962: 6).

When Rimbaud, in the same letter, counters René Descartes' humanistic 'I think, therefore I am' with the assertion that 'it is a mistake to say: I think. We should say: I am thought', he anticipates this key turn in post-Nietzschean thinking; but he continues to display in his own writing a fierce individualism and an unquenchable commitment to imaginative and political liberty. For Althusser, by contrast, the 'subject' of history is not the individual human being, speaking and acting purposively in a world illuminated by rational freedom, but the impersonal 'structure in dominance', what Marx called the 'forces and relations of production' that 'operate outside man and independent of his will', and that set the pattern and horizon of individual action. Others, though, have contended that Althusser, for all his flirtation with the vocabulary of 'structural' causation and his ascription of a structuralist *coupure* to the mature Marx, belongs, like Marx himself, in the turbulent mainstream of continental thinking, and that his antihumanism springs not from some irreversible Copernican rupture but from the long-running family quarrel of European philosophy with itself. He has even been accused, like a latter-day Comte, of a 'metaphysical passion for a system', whose Gallic single-mindedness 'threatens to obliterate' the complex realities of twentieth-century history. In this view,

> what appears disconcertingly unfamiliar or even indefinably alien ... becomes readily intelligible and identifiable when viewed against the background of European metaphysical philosophy, from Aristotle to Kant, and Nietzsche to Heidegger.
>
> (Stedman-Jones 1977: 314, 274)

But in spite of Thompson's energetic polemic and the scepticism of his fellow philosophers, Althusser's reputation and influence, in Britain and Europe at least, remained formidable for two decades or more, and helped to accelerate the antihumanist turn that has coloured most subsequent discussion in the social sciences and in what some still nostalgically call 'the humanities'. Barrett notes that, for many people, 'humanism' has become 'a code word for the "impotent" and reactionary values of the bourgeois literary canon builders of the eighteenth to twentieth centuries', with the consequence that 'in some circles *it is assumed* that "humanist" is a derogatory term' (Barrett 1991: 93).

At the same time, even as its theoretical stock crashed, the *rhetorical* repertoire of humanism continued to be used without embarrassment, even by the most intransigent antihumanists. Many young British Althusserians turned out to campaign against nuclear weapons, to support the mineworkers in the strike of 1983–4, to get rid of Mrs Thatcher's poll tax in 1989 – and to justify those campaigns in the name of the hallowed rights and liberties of speech, work and representation. Althusser himself accounts for this apparent contradiction by means of a strict distinction between *theory* (antihumanism) and *ideology* (humanism), the latter being, like the Royalists in the Civil War, 'wrong but wromantic'; or rather, philosophically disreputable but pragmatically necessary:

> it can serve as a *practical, ideological* slogan in so far as it is exactly adequate to its function and not confused with a quite different function; that there is no way in which it can abrogate the attributes of a *theoretical* concept.

> (Althusser 1969: 246)

The distinction between 'theory' and 'ideology' – between, in plain terms, knowledge and error – is important, and not to be scoffingly dismissed as a piffling pedantry. Indeed, it is central to the humanist project itself, as Althusser attests in his frequent comparison of Marx with Galileo. But for most people, it remains a purely *contemplative* distinction, and I doubt whether those caught up – in southern Africa, Eastern Europe, Latin America – in the struggle for national emancipation and political representation are detained by it for long. When Nelson Mandela called for a 'new reality' in South Africa, one that would 'reinforce humanity's belief in justice' and 'strengthen its confidence in the nobility of the human soul', not even Margaret Thatcher, who was still calling him a terrorist, demanded his arraignment before the international court of theoretical correctness (Mandela 1994: 41). In any case, it is far from clear, even this late in the day, that Althusser is right to conflate humanism with Stalinism, or to relegate it to the category of serviceable delusion, a new opium of the masses for a post-Christian age.

***

On 28 January 1975, eight professors of philosophy at the University of Belgrade were suspended from their posts. Outside their specialised and to most people incomprehensible discipline, philosophy professors are not generally regarded as figures of much historical significance, and the event went largely unnoticed. The British press was more concerned in the days that followed with the escapades of the absconding Labour politician John Stonehouse and the challenge for the Tory leadership from an ambitious outsider called Margaret Thatcher. But for the student of humanism, the incident is of some interest.

The eight were all members of the 'Praxis group', a regular seminar of Marxist intellectuals committed to the development and dissemination of a version of Marxism that differed sharply both from the Marxist-Leninist orthodoxy dominant in the Soviet imperium and its satellites and from the officially sanctioned Marxism of the ageing Tito's increasingly unstable and crisis-riven Yugoslavia. Official Marxism, grounded in the heroic triumphalism of *The Communist Manifesto* and the lapidary impersonality of *Capital*, insists on the inevitability and objectivity of the great historic forces that impel humanity towards the future. The forces and relations of production, in Marx's words, operate 'outside man and independent of his will' (Marx and Engels 1968: 180–84). The Praxis philosophers, in contrast, found in the earlier writings of Marx, and particularly in the recently translated 'Paris Manuscripts' of 1844, the possibility of a Marxism rooted not in the impersonal dynamics of class or social system but in a still unrealised conviction of human potentiality, agency and need. In their debates in the mid-1960s, the historian of the group has written, 'the view prevailed that the central category of Marx's philosophy was free, human, creative activity', and the problem for a socialist society they defined as 'how to realize human nature by producing a more humane world' (Markovic 1975: 23, 31). The analysis of alienation, the separation of human life from its own essential humanity, becomes 'the basic task of philosophy', and the problem for Marxists is

> to reconcile the principle of determinism, according to which historical processes are governed by laws independent of human consciousness and will, with the principle of freedom according to which it is men who make their own history.
>
> (ibid.: 18–19)

As a theoretical issue, the problem of reconciling historical necessity with human freedom remains unresolved. As a practical matter, at that time and place, the attempt to arbitrate it on 'the common ground of Marxist humanism' was almost certainly bound to fail. The socialist humanism of the Praxis group, which flourished briefly between 1964 and its enforced dismantlement in 1975, has a specially poignant significance in the brief and tragic history of the Yugoslav Republic, which for many European socialists, dismayed by the brutal posturings of cold-war super-states, seemed for a fugitive moment to hold out the hope of a 'communism with a human face'. Holding a precarious balance, as one of the group has written, between 'right-wing nationalists (especially in Croatia) and pro-Stalinist hardliners (especially in Serbia)' (Markovic 1975: 28), it must strike us in retrospect as pitiably vulnerable, doomed to be trampled heedlessly by the very historical forces it had sought to comprehend and humanise.

By the time its flame flickered briefly in the gathering darkness of Yugoslav repression, 'socialist humanism' had already served for two decades to rally dissident Marxists, within and outside the communist and socialist parties of eastern and western Europe. The historian Edward Thompson, who in 1957 founded and co-edited the *New Reasoner* ('A Quarterly Journal of Socialist Humanism'), calls it 'the motto of the Communist libertarian opposition in 1956' (the year in which the Soviet leadership for the first time criticised the Stalinist 'cult of personality', and sent Red Army tanks to put down the Hungarian uprising), and recalls that

> it arose simultaneously in a hundred places, and on ten thousand lips. It was voiced by poets in Poland, Russia, Hungary, Czechoslovakia; by factory delegates in Budapest; by Communist militants at the eighth plenum of the Polish Party; by a Communist premier (Imre Nagy), who was murdered for his pains. It was on the lips of women and men coming out of gaol and of the relatives and friends of those who never came out.
>
> (Thompson 1978: 322)

Thompson's eloquent and impassioned testimony to this movement is occasioned by his angry rebuttal of Althusser's 'theoretical anti-humanism'. He associates it particularly with 'the generation of the anti-fascist struggle and the Resistance', the generation of socialists which, to quote Thompson again,

> cut its teeth on the causes of Spain and of Indian independence, chewed on a World War ... and has been offered an international diet ever since – Yugoslavia and Bulgaria, the Peace Movement and the Korean War, and thence to '1956', Suez, Cyprus, Algeria, Cuba, Vietnam, Chile.
>
> (Thompson 1978: iii)

This is also the generation that, in Britain, voted a Labour government into power in 1945; and their children, the 'angry young men' (and women) who rejected the servile complacencies and stale pieties of post-war respectability, and found a public voice in the writing of young socialists and humanists like John Arden, Arnold Wesker, Shelagh Delaney, Trevor Griffiths and Edward Bond; the generation whose sleeping and waking nightmares were haunted by those malignant icons of twentieth-century inhumanity, the extermination camp and the atomic bomb. Bond, in particular, articulates a humanistic socialism that evokes, in its confident generalisation of the human and its unshaken faith in the power of progressive reason, the universalising discourse of enlightenment:

> An artist cannot create art, cannot demonstrate his objective truth, in the service of reaction or fascism; because art is not merely the discovery of new truth or new aspects of old truth – but also the demonstration of the human need for the rational ... Art isn't the discovery of particular truths in the way science is; it also demonstrates the practical working out of the human need for truth.
>
> (Bond 1978: xv)

The 'human need for the rational' is fundamental – biological – for Bond; and the struggle of humanity to emancipate itself, which is the true subject of all authentic art, is history, a concept endowed with a positively Hegelian purposiveness and rationality:

> this is the reason that our understanding of the art of the past is often better than artists' contemporaries. The truth of art may be

described as 'viability'. Tyranny and injustice aren't 'viable'; they can
be lived with but not expressed with consent and approval in art –
that is, made normative. Viable in this context means expressing the
rationality of history.

(ibid.: xvii)

The unabashed historicism and rationalism of this, written in
1978, is a useful caution against attributing too wide an influence
to the ideas of Althusser and his British enthusiasts, since Bond
is clearly quite untouched by – or indifferent to – the fulminations of theoretical antihumanism. As so often before, the appeal
to the 'human need for truth' invokes the familiar Greek model:
'Greek artists wrote about men and society as objectively as they
could: that is, they wrote rationally'. But although Bond, a post-war
Marxist who quotes Adorno's embargo on poetry after Auschwitz,
is well aware of the dangers that lurk within the 'dialectic of
enlightenment', his rational meliorism, which offers itself as a
method of change' rather than a coercive 'plan of the future'
(ibid.: 11), betrays few misgivings about the humanist project
itself. He has written with uninhibited eloquence against apartheid,
nuclear weapons, the British occupation of Northern Ireland and
(in *Lear*, his finest play) Stalinist tyranny, and has a strong claim
to have produced the most impressive body of work inspired by
Marxist humanism since the poet and designer William Morris,
author of the socialist utopia *News from Nowhere* (1891).

And yet, as Thompson (whose first book was a fine study of
Morris) himself acknowledges, 'socialist humanism', mobilised in
1956 as 'the voice of a Communist opposition, of a total critique
of Stalinist practice and theory', has a complex and ambiguous
lineage of its own. For Stalinism had itself already laid claim to
the term: borrowing the title of a famous essay by Maxim Gorky,
Soviet communism would be a 'proletarian humanism', at once
the fulfilment and the transcendence of the humanist project.
Writing from Moscow in 1936, and addressing the socialist and
communist parties of the European 'Popular Front' as well as the
ideological constabulary of Soviet cultural orthodoxy, the Hungarian Marxist Georg Lukács had already contrasted the contemplative, nonpolitical liberalism of Stefan Zweig, whose study

of the fifteenth-century Dutch humanist Erasmus 'emptied humanism of all revolutionary-democratic content and therewith degraded it to a wearisome, bourgeois and liberal respectability' (Lukács 1969: 320), with the 'humanist protest' of western intellectuals against the 'imperialist barbarism' of German and Italian fascism, as evidenced in the novels of Lion Feuchtwanger, Thomas Mann and his brother Heinrich, and the French socialist Romain Rolland, and looked forward to a renaissance of popular historical fiction under the banner of 'democratic humanism', a development in which 'of course the model of the Soviet Union plays a big part' (ibid.: 318). 'A living form of humanism', as he wrote on another occasion,

> prepares [readers] to endorse the political slogans of the Popular Front and to comprehend its political humanism. Through the mediation of realist literature the soul of the masses is made receptive for an understanding of the great, progressive and democratic epochs of human history.
>
> (Lukács et al. 1971: 156–57)

Lukács, a classically educated German-speaking Magyar deeply imbued with the values of nineteenth-century *Bildung*, whose private opinion of Stalin's Russia is betrayed by his barely lukewarm enthusiasm for the achievements of 'socialist realism' and his coded 'Aesopian' critique of Stalinist orthodoxy, stopped short of calling Soviet communism a 'revolutionary humanism', a phrase he reserved for the popular movements of the nineteenth century. Indeed, his warning, directed to his Russian as much as his western readers, that 'any Utopian anticipation of the future, any transformation of the future into a supposed reality can very easily cause a slipping back into the style of the period of decline' (Lukács 1969: 422) comes as close as was possible to identifying Stalinism with the philistine military autocracy of Bismarck's Germany. But most of Lukács' fellow apparatchiks were not sophisticated readers, and his carefully worded assertion that 'a new historical novel, born of the popular and democratic spirit of our time', is now a possibility 'not only for the writers of the Soviet Union, but also for the humanists of the anti-Fascist popular front' (ibid.: 420) could easily be read, and was perhaps intended to be read, as a proclamation of uncritical solidarity.

These equivocations were costly, and Lukács, in whose defence it can at least be pleaded that they were the price of survival, was very far from being the only western intellectual to give his imprimatur to the idea that the Soviet Union had at last consummated the humanist dream of universal rational freedom. In 1960, back in Budapest and reprinting *The Historical Novel* for a western readership (the original 1937 edition had been in Russian), he was prepared to admit (in German) that 'my political perspective of the time proved too optimistic', an elegantly noncommittal way to acknowledge the show-trials and assassinations of political opponents, and the liquidation of millions of obstinate peasants and dissident intellectuals, while continuing to insist, with the Soviet invasion of his native Hungary still fresh in memory, that 'this in no way alters the significance of the theoretical questions raised and the direction in which their solution is to be sought' (Lukács 1969: 10).

Similar equivocations characterise the thinking of Lukács' Russian contemporaries in the decade following Stalin's death in 1952. While conceding, with perhaps a touch of understatement, that 'the conditions created by the cult of Stalin's personality inevitably affected the theoretical elaboration of the problems of humanism in the USSR' (Petrosyan 1972: 12), one representative missal of Soviet orthodoxy declared (in 1964) that:

> Humanism pervades the entire spiritual world of Soviet man, is its essence and is expressed in morality, moral goals, devotion to communism, understanding of man's purpose, the meaning of life, happiness and duty, in the sense of moral responsibility towards the people and mankind, in comradely mutual assistance, internationalism, and implacable hostility towards the enemies of communism, peace and the freedom of the peoples.
>
> (Petrosyan 1972: 286)

What this liturgy of banalities demonstrates is that Belgrade 1975, like the far bloodier confrontations of Prague 1968 and

Budapest 1956, was no simple morality play, a courageous few raising the humanist standard against the armed inhumanity of Stalinist hegemony. The obduracies and compromises of socialist humanism leave no room for complacency or naïveté. Like Lukács and Petrosyan, and indeed Stalin himself, the university authorities were good humanists too, though they wore their humanism at a different angle from their colleagues in the philosophy faculty. What was at issue, with grave consequences for poor, doomed Yugoslavia, was, as always, a contest of humanisms, a struggle ('which is to be master – that's all') for the ownership and definition of the word.

THE DEATH OF MAN

If Althusser's essays helped to dislodge the tenacious hold of humanist assumptions about the autonomy and integrity of the individual, and to establish the idea of human beings not as free agents but as points of contingency for the impersonal historical forces of class struggle and ideology, the antihumanist turn is seen at its most radical in the work of his compatriot Michel Foucault. For not only does Althusser concede that the language of human individuality and solidarity must for the foreseeable future retain at least a pragmatic efficacy; his own writing, for all its theoretical severity, serves frankly humanist ends of enlightenment and emancipation. For Foucault, not only is humanism a limited and outmoded philosophy; its central conception of 'man', now exposed as never much more, in any case, than a grammatical convenience, is due for the scrapyard.

> One thing in any case is certain: man is neither the oldest nor the most constant problem that has been posed for human knowledge. Taking a relatively short chronological sample within a restricted geographical area – European culture since the sixteenth century – one can be certain that man is a recent invention within it ... As the archaeology of our thought easily shows, man is an invention of recent date. And one perhaps nearing its end.
>
> (Foucault 1970: 386–87)

This passage is from the closing pages of *The Order of Things* (*Les mots et les choses*), his first book, based, like Nietzsche's *Birth of Tragedy*, on his boldly unconventional doctoral thesis; and his subsequent writings develop the critique of the concept 'man' through a deconstructive archaeology of the dominant 'discourses' within which its authority was constructed: the psychiatric discourse of the 'mad' and the 'sane', the penological discourse of the 'criminal', above all the discourse of sexual normality and deviance. *Discourse* for Foucault is what the relations of production are for Marx, the unconscious for Freud, the impersonal laws of language for Saussure, ideology for Althusser: the capillary structure of social cohesion and conformity. Discourse situates us as individuals, and silently legislates the boundaries of what is possible for us to think and say. Above all, it is normative: not in the sense that transgression and dissent are impossible, for Foucault is less interested in coercion and prohibition than in 'liberal' modes of regulation like psychiatry, open prisons, sexual 'permissiveness', but because they too are 'grammatical', already anticipated and mapped into the hegemonic syntax of discursive power.

Foucault acknowledged the inspiration of Nietzsche, more radical in his view than either Marx or Freud. Following his mentor's 'exegesis of a few Greek words' (1970: 298), his later writings on sexuality took him to Hellenic antiquity (Foucault 1986). But his major work was on the archaeology of the modern, the life-span of post-Renaissance 'man', a figure first fully articulated in the writings of 'enlightened' eighteenth-century freethinkers and *philosophes* like Hume, Kant and Diderot, and whose origins are to be found not in ancient Greece but in the fifteenth-century Italian cities about which Burckhardt and Symonds wrote, and on whose behalf they constructed a historical narrative of epochal scope and energy, a story of ancient continuities lost and found again, of Promethean feats of discovery and conquest, of an infant humanism that could not yet speak its name.

3

HUMANISTS BEFORE HUMANISM

What a piece of work is a man!

(*Hamlet*)

He who swims in our sea has no shore but himself.

(Abu Ya'qub al-Sijistani)

For their Victorian enthusiasts, the early humanists were adventurers, as fearless in their explorations of the intellectual world as their seafaring contemporaries were in the discovery and conquest of the physical one. Symonds called the Florentine scholar-poet Francesco Petrarca (Petrarch) 'the Columbus of a new spiritual hemisphere, the discoverer of modern culture' (1898: 62). Walter Pater described the Renaissance as 'that movement in which, in various ways, the human mind wins for itself a new kingdom of feeling and sensation and thought' (1873: 54). This is the language of colonisation and empire, conscripting the earlier humanists to the commercial, scientific and imperial expansionism of the later nineteenth century.

Most of the early humanists, in contrast, saw their task not as the *discovery* of the future but as the *recovery* of the past. Although it was inspired by, and refers directly to, the transatlantic voyages of the Florentine adventurer Amerigo Vespucci, what is interesting about Thomas More's *Utopia* (1516) is how un-futuristic it all seems, its peaceful, equitable community combining a monastic simplicity of life with the imagined tranquillity of a long-forgotten golden age. When Christopher Marlowe's humanistic Faustus boasts that he has 'made blind Homer sing to me' (Marlowe 1969: 285), it is a gesture not of revolutionary iconoclasm but of poignant archaeological homage and reversionary longing, harnessing the ancient arts of magic – the *Cabbala*, the occult texts of the legendary Egyptian magus Hermes Trismegistus – to raise the slumbering spirit of the founding patriarch of European poetry. Petrarch, who modelled his conduct, like his prose style, on the Roman philosopher-statesman Marcus Tullius Cicero, expressed his feelings about the 'modern culture' whose discovery Symonds burdens him with by dressing in private in a senatorial toga and conversing in Latin, and not the degenerate dog-Latin of the monks, but the pure idiom of his beloved Tully. 'What is it to be a Florentine,' asked his friend Coluccio Salutati, 'except to be, both by nature and law, a Roman citizen?' (Dickens 1972: 14). And in one of his private letters, Niccolò Machiavelli describes how, after a day working in the fields of his Tuscan farm,

> I return to my home and enter my study; and at the door I take off the day's clothing, covered with mud and dust, and put on garments regal and courtly; and reclothed appropriately, I enter the ancient courts of ancient men, where, received by them with affection, I feed on that food which only is mine and which I was born for, where I am not ashamed to speak with them and to ask them the reasons for their actions; and they in their kindness [*umanità*] answer me; and for four hours of time I do not feel boredom, I forget every trouble, I do not dread poverty, I am not frightened by death; entirely I give myself over to them.
>
> (Machiavelli 1961: 142)

Petrarch, Salutati, Machiavelli, More: the founding figures of European humanism were adventurers, no doubt; but the new world they sought lay in the past, not the future. In a more, and more literally, pedestrian sense, however, the humanists of the fourteenth, fifteenth and sixteenth centuries were travellers. Early humanism was not, in the sense that later 'isms' like socialism or pacifism or feminism are, a 'movement'; indeed, it was not, before the nineteenth century, an 'ism' at all; but it was certainly *in* movement, created and disseminated by people on the move. From the Byzantine Greek Manolis Chrysoloras, who began to teach his native language to the children of Florentine merchants in 1397, to the English poet John Milton, whose humanist interests were ripened by his travels in France and Italy in 1638–9, the itinerant *umanisti* and their patrons, students and enthusiasts created an informal peripatetic network of personal discussion, correspondence and conviviality which conveyed ideas, languages and (most importantly) books to schools, universities, private collections and solitary scholars across the European continent and its islands. Humanist writing in the period conveys the pleasures and discomforts of travel, by boat, on foot, on horse-back, no less than the excitements of intellectual discovery, especially the discomforts, as evoked in Thomas More's description of his friend Desiderius Erasmus trudging

> through dense forest and wild woodland, over rugged hilltops and steep mountains, along roads beset with bandits ... tattered by the winds, spattered with mud, travel-weary, worn out by hardships.
>
> (More 1961: 137)

Not many ventured as far afield as the fifteenth-century anti-quarian Cyriac of Ancona, who tutored the Ottoman sultan Mehmet II, conqueror of Constantinople, in Greek and Roman literature, and whose illustrated journals preserve the details of hundreds of ancient buildings, inscriptions and works of art throughout Greece, Turkey and the Middle East. Fewer still sought to rival the Catholic humanist Matteo Ricci, founder of the Jesuit mission in Beijing, who adopted Chinese dress, life-style and even name (Li-ma-teu), and through whose translations European readers first discovered the writings of the 'Chinese Socrates' Kung-fu-tzu, together with his Latinised name, Confucius.

But all along the principal land and sea routes between northern and Mediterranean Europe, informal genealogies of humanist collaboration can be traced across two centuries and more. The ten-year-old Milton learnt Latin, Greek and Hebrew under Alexander Gill at St Paul's School, within a curriculum substantially unchanged since its principles had been laid down a hundred years earlier by the school's founder John Colet. Colet, like the school's first headmaster William Lily, author of a famous Latin *Grammar* that was still in use in Milton's day, had studied in Florence and Rome in the early 1490s, and his pioneering lectures at Oxford University in the later 1490s on the Epistles of St Paul drew on the discoveries of his Dutch friend Erasmus, who himself had studied Greek and the editing of ancient authors with the pioneering printer Aldo Manuzio in Venice, developing the work of the itinerant Roman scholar Lorenzo Valla in applying the linguistic and critical skills of humanist scholarship to the text of the New Testament, skills which Valla had himself acquired from Florentine Greeks in the 1430s.

On occasion, as the example of St Paul's School indicates, this informal network of vagrant intellectuals could precipitate itself, with help from a powerful patron, into an institution. By the middle of the sixteenth century, schools or colleges teaching Greek, Latin and Hebrew (hence sometimes called 'trilingual') within a humanist curriculum had been established not only in Paris (the Collège de France, 1530), London (Westminster, 1560, as well as St Paul's), Oxford (Corpus Christi College, 1517) and Cambridge (St John's College, 1511), but also in provincial towns such as Birmingham (King Edward's School, 1552), Ipswich (Thomas Wolsey's Cardinal's College, 1528), Bordeaux (the Collège de Guyenne, 1534), Wittenberg (now the Martin Luther University, 1502), Louvain (the Catholic University, 1425) and Alcalá (the great Universidad Complutense, 1499), as well as countless small private schools of the kind that Milton himself set up on his return to England in 1639. But in general the relations between the majority of *umanisti*, and their position within the major institutions of intellectual authority, remained fluid and often precarious. And just as 'humanism' has no consistent meaning (indeed, no linguistic existence) in the period, so the humanists, whether teachers, scholars, patrons, publishers or wealthy amateurs of the 'new learning', had no common programme of interests or objectives. Indeed, whether because of the transient insecurity of their lives, the formidable power of the political and religious institutions with which they often found themselves in conflict, or the critical and contentious character of the humanist inclination itself, the relations between leading humanists were notable as much for their acrimonious fallings out as for their lasting friendships. For all that, friendship, rather than allegiance to a shared ideological or intellectual programme, remains the ideal humanist relationship, finding its model in the private letters and the *De amicitia* ('On Friendship') of Cicero and, sometimes, in the homoerotic subculture of the Platonic dialogues, and its practical embodiment in the argumentative hospitality of the 'sodality', a sort of quasi-monastic hostel-cum-debating society where a travelling scholar could find a bed, a meal and congenial company for a week or two.

HUMANIST PRINTING

Even more than the schools, the universities and the casual associations of itinerant intellectuals, though, the key humanist institution is the printing shop. Without the invention of movable type and the establishment of independent printing houses, the new learning, its key texts available only in laborious, expensive and inaccurate manuscript copies, would have remained the preserve of the wealthy patron, the scholarly specialist and above all the Church. Where manuscript production was slow, costly and, since most copyists were monks, monopolised by the Church and the universities, print was fast, cheaper and widely available. The great manuscript libraries were aristocratic or clerical. Book buyers were, on the whole, middle class and lay.

The revolutionary implications of movable type were obvious from the outset. Perhaps through a confusion between the fifteenth-century printer and entrepreneur Johann Fust and the celebrated magician Johann Georg Faust, the tradition developed that printing was the invention of the devil. Milton compared it to the dragon's teeth from which Cadmus, legendary founder of Thebes and supposed inventor of the alphabet, raised an army from the barren soil (Milton 1990: 578). 'Thanks to printed letters,' wrote Rousseau, 'the dangerous daydreams of a Hobbes and a Spinoza will last for ever' (Smeed 1975: 49). The leading fifteenth- and sixteenth-century humanist printers, generally known by the Latin form of their names that appeared on their title pages, were also publishers, booksellers and scholars, and above all entrepreneurs with a commercial as well as a cultural interest in the widest possible distribution of books; and they presided in turn over a workforce of compositors, proofreaders, binders, illustrators, editors and commentators, every one of whom needed to be a proficient reader not only of their mother tongue but of Latin, Greek and probably Hebrew too. The leading print-shops were in effect mini-polytechnics of humanist knowledge, offering instruction in practical skills such as type design and composition, textual collation and editing, as well as first-hand contact with the literature of Mediterranean antiquity. The doyen of humanist printer-publishers, the Venetian Teobaldo Manuzio (Aldus Manutius), whose Cretan type-founders produced the first Greek and italic fonts (the latter said to have been modelled on Petrarch's handwriting), employed the young Erasmus and the French humanist Guillaume Budé in this way at his famous Aldine press in Venice. François Rabelais worked in the Lyon print-shop of the expatriate German Sebastian Gryphius. The Estienne (Stephanus) brothers, Robert and Henri, offered similar opportunities to aspiring scholars in Paris and later Geneva.

But the expansion and influence of printing in the later fifteenth century went far beyond the handful of big names (Aldus, Gryphius, the Stephani, Henry Frobenius in Basle, Christopher Plantin in Antwerp). The scale and speed of the revolution can be gauged by the fact that by 1500, less than half a century after Gutenberg started printing in Mainz and only twenty-five years after Caxton set up his first press in Bruges, there were fifty print-shops in Lyon alone, with a comparable expansion in every sizeable town in continental Europe: not only the great metropoles of political and ecclesiastical power, but the commercial centres and major crossroads of international trade like Augsburg, Rouen, Parma, Lüneburg and Antwerp.

ELOQUENCE AND IDENTITY

The *umanità* of Machiavelli's ancient companions, the generosity with which, conjured by the necromancy of the printed page, their voices respond to the urgent promptings of the modern Florentine, is inseparable from the language in which those voices speak. For humanism, at this time, is above all a question of language, and the oddly ambivalent antiquarianism of these pioneers of the old emerges most clearly in their highly equivocal attitude towards the vernacular languages of their own time. Machiavelli's letter, like the books which made him famous, or infamous, *The Prince* and the *Discourses* on the works of the Roman historian Titus Livius, is written in Italian. So are the *Rime* ('rhymes'), the three-hundred-odd sonnets and canzoni that made Petrarch one of the most influential figures in fifteenth- and sixteenth-century writing. In this, they both follow the example of their fellow-Florentine Dante Alighieri, whose *Divine Comedy* is the first major European poem in a modern language, and who in *De vulgari eloquentia*, a Latin treatise arguing for the creation of a vernacular literature, urges poets to honour the ancients not by slavishly imitating their language but by doing what they did, developing a literary idiom out of the spoken language of their own compatriots.

The wide circulation and secular accessibility of print point, too, to the advantages of vernacular literacy. Yet many early humanists viewed these opportunities with an ambivalence verging on revulsion. Not many went as far as the father of the young Michel de Montaigne, who made all the farmhands and domestics on his estate learn Latin so that the boy should have no need to descend to the vulgarity of French (in later life, Montaigne even swore in Latin). But a certain suspicion of the vernacular, and in particular of the fluidity and hybridity of spoken language, underpins the humanist project. Dante's argument for vernacular literature had insisted that all the existing spoken vernaculars of Italy and France were worse than useless to a serious writer, and that a literary language, 'illustrious, cardinal, courtly and curial', would have to be refined out of the base metal of everyday speech (Alighieri 1981: 34). For humanists, too, the model of linguistic purity is classical Latin and Greek, and even those writers who chose or were compelled, for commercial or ideological reasons, to write in a modern language generally sought to create a literary idiom as remote as possible from contemporary speech, a kind of classical vernacular. The scholarly printer Henri Estienne (Henricus Stephanus) argued in his *Traité de la conformité du langage français avec le grec* (1564) that French was the purest of all modern languages because it was the closest to ancient Greek; and Edmund Spenser, who deplored the mongrelised English of his time as 'a gallimaufray or hodgepodge of al other speches' (Spenser 1912: 417), devised for his own *Shepheardes Calendar* (1579) a learned and pseudo-archaic idiom intended to evoke the language of Chaucer, the 'English Homer', and behind him the classical Latin of Virgil's *Eclogues*.

Above all, early humanism is a question of language because of its central preoccupation with *eloquence*. The Latin word *eloquentia* means 'speaking out', and encompasses, certainly, the sort of thing we mean by 'public speaking': the oratorical skills of the preacher or politician, advocate or entertainer. The humanist curriculum placed much emphasis on such skills, viewing knowledge as inert and occluded until shared and tested in the common medium of written or spoken debate. But eloquence has a deeper and more intimate relation to the humanist conception of self. If man is (in a definition often attributed to Aristotle) the 'speaking animal', then we exist most fully not in the intimate interiority of private thought and feeling but in the communality of linguistic exchange. 'Language most shows a man', wrote Ben Jonson, in a vivid phrase borrowed from the Spanish humanist Juan Luis Vives: 'Speak, that I may see thee' (Jonson 1975: 435). Indeed, the very notion of a 'private self', so fundamental to romantic and later conceptions of identity, is alien to early humanist thinking. The human animal is fashioned and defined in language, and belongs inseparably, in its public and private aspects alike, to the medium of discourse.

In truth, though, simple oppositions like public and private, objective and subjective, form and content, won't take us very far in this context. Nothing, for example, could be more 'public', more impersonal, than printing: the mechanised manufacture of large numbers of identical commodities for profitable sale to a 'reading public' whose individual identities are a matter of complete indifference to the writers and other producers of those objects. Yet in the production of those commodities, and even more in their silent and solitary consumption, quite unprecedented depths and ardours of privacy, of intimate colloquy and self-communing inwardness are disclosed. The complex web of relations between writers, readers and characters, so potently charged with subjective warmth and fantasy, is wholly contingent upon an economy of cold commercial exchange whose principal agents, printers, compositors, booksellers, remain virtually nameless and invisible.

Even so, dependent though it is upon the anonymity and mechanical objectivity of print and the silent interiority of private reading, early humanism is all talk: voluble, intimate, opinionated. Like its own favourite reading matter, the dialogues of Plato and Xenophon, the letters of Cicero and the satires of Horace, humanist discourse dissolves writing itself into the relaxed conviviality of conversation. Rhetorical precepts derived from Aristotle and the Roman rhetorician Quintilian may seek to restrain its exuberance and codify its expressive repertoire into a copy-book of abstract 'tropes'; but eloquence, even at its most formal, is always transitive: it intends to persuade, bully, cajole or impress someone in particular. It discovers, in the heat of argumentative and didactic utterance as in the cool manipulations of movable type, fresh configurations of subjectivity, new ways of thinking and feeling the self.

Take two of the most famous and influential of early humanist texts. In the first of these, an English lawyer, visiting Antwerp on political business, is introduced by a Flemish friend to a Portuguese traveller, recently returned from the East Indies. The three retire to the Englishman's lodgings, where they sit in the garden while the traveller describes the inhabitants and curious customs of a previously unknown island he has discovered on his travels. In the evening they part, promising to resume their conversation on another occasion.

This bald summary is not, of course, intended to give any impression of the substantial content of Thomas More's *Utopia*, published (in Latin) in 1516; but it does serve to bring out the most striking formal feature of humanist writing: its devotion to dialogue. Plato is the major model, especially, for More, the *Republic* and the *Laws*; but humanist dialogue is more contentious and open-ended than its Platonic counterpart, lacking the authoritative Socratic voice, and counterpointing seriousness and eloquent intensity with deflationary turns of irony, scepticism and humour. The traveller Hythlodaeus's account of the peaceable communistic society of the Utopians, where 'no men are poor, no men are beggars, and though no man owns anything, everyone is rich', like his impassioned denunciation of contemporary society as 'nothing but a conspiracy of the rich, who are fattening up their own interests under the name and title of the commonwealth' (More 1989: 107–8), is framed and ironised by the polite scepticism of his companion, the fictional (but authorial) 'Morus', a scepticism he shares with the reader but not with the utopian enthusiast himself, who, he sees,

> was tired with talking, and I was not sure he could take contradiction in these matters, particularly when I recalled what he had said about certain counsellors who were afraid they might not appear knowing enough unless they found something to criticise in other men's ideas. So with praise for the Utopian way of life and his account of it, I took him by the hand and led him in to supper.
>
> (More 1989: 110)

The demands of hospitality can conflict with those of absolute honesty, and friendship may at times require an urbane dissimulation. Even the controversial humanist must sometimes admit the dangers of controversy.

The overlapping ironies of *Utopia*, whose Greek title can mean both 'good place' and 'no place', have divided readers ever since, and this most famous example of the genre which has borrowed its title has been hijacked by quite incompatible critical and ideological persuasions, having been claimed as a blueprint for communism, for social-democratic reformism, for neo-medievalist conservatism, and as a satire on all political idealisms (Morton 1978: 76). Where, such readers ask, is More himself in his text? Is he the idealist Hythlodaeus, the principal speaker, with his savage critique of early capitalism and Tudor *Realpolitik*? Or the sceptical Morus, to whom he has given his own name, and who finds 'quite a few of the laws and customs he had described as existing among the Utopians ... really absurd' (More 1989: 110)? Or is he – the classic position of the beleaguered liberal – somewhere between the two? The text's most recent editors find in it the expression of a 'divided, complex mind – capable of seeing more than one side of a question and reluctant to make a definite commitment to any single position' (ibid.: xxi). But it may be more helpful to see in the book's famous ironies and discontinuities evidence not of authorial uncertainty or agnosticism but rather of the indefatigable openness of the dialogical mode itself, within which the anxiety for certainty and closure is constantly frustrated by the tantalising provisionality of humanist debate. There is always something more to be said, and no speaker enjoys the privilege of the last word:

> So with praise for the Utopian way of life and his account of it, I took him by the hand and led him in to supper. But first I said that we would find some other time for thinking of these matters more deeply, and for talking them over in more detail. And I still hope such an opportunity will present itself some day.
>
> (More 1989: 110)

In my second of these characteristic and influential texts, set a few years later and a thousand miles or so to the south of Antwerp, some members of a papal entourage have decided, on their way home from a successful mission to Mantua, to break their journey for a few days at the court of Urbino, where they can spend their evenings discussing love, war and other matters with the learned, hospitable Duchess and her friends. Like *Utopia*, Baldassare Castiglione's *Book of the Courtier* (*Il libro del cortegiano*, 1528) weaves a fictional dialogue around actual people and events. Once again the primary model is Platonic, in this case the discussion of love in the *Symposium*. Like More's book, too, it has its genial ironies and unexpected turns. In the fourth book, the philosopher Pietro Bembo's rhapsodic invocation to love bursts the ripe grape of neoplatonic eloquence, dissolving its passionate earnestness into laughter:

> When Bembo had hitherto spoken with such vehemency, that a man would have thought him (as it were) ravished and beside himself, he stood still without once moving, holding his eyes toward heaven as astonied: when the Lady Emilia, which together with the rest gave most diligent ear to this talk, took him by the plait of his garment, and plucking him a little said 'Take heed (master Peter) that these thoughts make not your soul also to forsake the body.' 'Madam,' answered master Peter, 'it should not be the first miracle that love hath wrought in me.'

> (Castiglione 1928: 322)

Here again, the reversion from rapt monologue to humorous dialogue reopens issues: in this case, the question of gender, calling into debate the claimed universality of the Christian-Platonist discourse of love, and disclosing its underlying misogyny.

> 'Surely,' quoth the Duchess, 'if the not young Courtier be such a one, that he can follow this way which you have showed him, of right he ought to be satisfied with so great a happiness, and not to envy the younger.' Then the Lord Cesare Gonzaga, 'the way' (quoth he) 'that leadeth to this happiness is so steep (in my mind) that (I believe) it will be much ado to get to it.' The Lord Gaspar said: 'I believe it be hard to get up for men, but unpossible for women.' The Lady Emilia laughed and said: 'if ye fall so often to offend us, I promise you, ye shall be no more forgiven.'

> (Castiglione 1928: 322–23)

And here, too, the debate ends, or rather pauses, inconclusively, with the promise of a resumption and resolution that will never come:

> Whereupon they all taking their leave with reverence of the Duchess, departed toward their lodgings without torch, the light of the day sufficing. And as they were now passing out of the great Chamber door, the Lord General turned him to the Duchess, and said: 'Madam, to take up the variance between the Lord Gasper and the Lord Julian, we will assemble this night with the judge sooner than we did yesterday.'

> (Castiglione 1928: 423)

There, in the half-light of an Apennine dawn in early spring, with the first stirring of a morning breeze 'that filling the air with a biting cold, began to quicken the tunable notes of the pretty birds, among the hushing woods of the hills at hand', the dialogue ends.

Sir Thomas Hoby's lively, wayward translation of Castiglione, *The Courtyer*, published in 1561, informs a good deal of English writing in the later sixteenth century. It gave wide currency to the eroticised neoplatonic spirituality of Bembo's rhapsody, and helped to establish, in the figure of the ideal courtier, a particular humanist model of conduct, characterised by the quality that Castiglione calls *sprezzatura*. Later commentators have sentimentalised this concept, taking it to mean something like 'easy gracefulness'; but the root-word *sprezzare* means 'to despise', and Hoby's 'recklessness', with its implication of stylish indifference to danger, difficulty or conventional opinion, may be closer to the studied insouciance, the coolly disdainful virtuosity of 'the courtier's, soldier's, scholar's, eye, tongue, sword' (*Hamlet*, III, 1, 154):

> But I, imagining with my self often times how this grace commeth, leaving apart such as have it from above, find one rule that is most general, which in this part (me think) taketh place in all things belonging to a man in word or deed, above all other. And that is to eschew as much as a man may, and as a sharp and dangerous rock, too much curiousness, and (to speak a new word) to use in every thing a certain disgracing to cover art withall, and seem whatsoever he doth and saith, to do it without pain, and (as it were) not minding it. ... This virtue therefore contrary to curiosity, which we for this

time term Recklessness, beside that it is the true fountain from the which all grace springeth, it bringeth with it also another ornament, which accompanying any deed that a man doth, how little so ever it be, doth not only by and by open the knowledge of him that doth it, but also many times maketh it to be esteemed much more in effect than it is.

(Castiglione 1928: 45–49)

The distinction between action and contemplation, or, commonly, the tripartite schema of action, contemplation and passion, is pivotal to humanist conceptions of self; and it would be easy to link this reckless accomplishment with the active life, Bembo's spiritualised love of beauty with the passionate and contemplative, the pair forming together an ideal of unity and fulfilment. But there are interesting tensions. The courtier's elegantly studied recklessness is clearly, and exclusively, a masculine quality, emulative and, for all its seeming carelessness, strenuously imitative:

He therefore that will be a good scholar, beside the practising of good things must evermore set all his diligence to be like his master, and (if it were possible) change himself into him. And when he hath had some entry, it profiteth him much to behold sundry men of that profession: and governing himself with that good judgment that must always be his guide, go about to pick out, sometime of one, and sometime of another, sundry matters.

(Castiglione 1928: 45)

Love, on the other hand, encompasses and values, if only metaphorically, the idea of the feminine ('beauty'). Women's voices (the Duchess Elizabeth, her wittily unconventional friend Emilia Pia) cannot be excluded from its discourse, whose meanings will always be unstable, as the sardonic interpolations of the young misogynist Gasparo Pallavicino, for whom love is not only feminine but contemptibly effeminate, make clear. Proffered as an ideal of human fullness, the humanist courtier becomes instead a figure of discord, articulating the contradictions of aristocratic masculinity.

GENDER TROUBLE

Those contradictions surface irrepressibly in humanist writing, troubling its most intimate concerns and infiltrating the very grain and fibre of its language. One of the most active humanists in England in the later sixteenth century was the London-born, Oxford-educated Italian John (Giovanni) Florio. A lexicographer (he compiled the first English–Italian dictionary), translator (of the *Essais* of the French humanist Montaigne), language teacher and minor courtier, on friendly terms with Philip Sidney, Fulke Greville, Samuel Daniel and Ben Jonson, Florio did much to popularise the idiom and intellectual culture of the Florentine academies in England; and the long final chapter of his very entertaining *Second Frutes* (1591), a bilingual phrasebook for students of Italian, is, like book four of the *Courtier*, a nocturnal dialogue between friends 'wherein proverbially and pleasantly discourse is held of love, and of women'. To Silvestro's Bembo-like idealisation of love and womanly beauty, Pandolpho responds with an equally conventional, and equally humanist, misogyny, denouncing women as

> the most imperfect creatures, the errors of nature, the fall of man, the devil's bait, the subject of all vices, and cause, yea the very efficient cause of infinite calamities.
>
> (Florio 1591: 173)

This is familiar stuff, cut whole-cloth from a centuries-old tradition, sanctified by the Church and homespun prejudice, of antifeminist defamation. What raises the dialogue above the commonplace is Florio's recognition that the dialectics of sex saturate not only the discourses but the very medium of humanist eloquence, language itself. Taking a hint from Pandolpho's assertion that 'words are Feminine, & deedes are Masculine', Silvestro launches into an impassioned philological defence of the feminine:

> but tell me in good sooth, are not vices [*il vitio*] masculine, and virtues [*la virtù*] feminine? are not the Muses the love of the learned?

and do not Gentlemen follow the graces? not because Muses, nor because graces, but because women. There is but one Phoenix in the world, and she a Female ... Do you not see I pray you how the best creatures, & perfectest things that God hath created for the health, procreation & preservation of all his human creatures are of the feminine kind [del feminino genere], & are called women? For so it hath seemed good to all philosophers, lovers of learning, and searchers of sciences to name them ... The Bible [la bibbia], endited by the holy ghost, and written by the prophets, patriarchs, Evangelists, & Apostles, is a woman ... the liberal, prodigal and universal mother, and producer of all things and breathing creatures, that is to say earth [la terra], who with so bounteous a hand feeds all living things is a woman, and so are all her plants, her spices, her fruits, and fairest flowers.

(Florio 1591: 179, 199–201)

This paean to the female should not of course be confused with what we would now call feminism. All the authoritative figures in it, the 'philosophers, lovers of learning, and searchers of sciences' who name the world, the 'prophets, patriarchs, Evangelists, & Apostles' who write its scriptures, the speakers in the dialogue, the author himself, are male. Misogyny and philogyny, hatred and idealisation of women, are equally and inseparably elements of the male discourse of eloquence, men speaking of and for women.

But the relation between them is textually unstable. The elision, typical in humanist writing, of the grammatical into the cultural-biological senses of gender licenses a good deal of confusion and rhetorical opportunism. Which is the true face of virtue, Silvestro's feminised *virtù* or Machiavelli's sternly masculine appropriation of the same word, which some translations of *The Prince* gloss as 'manliness'? But it also points towards contradictions and instabilities deep within the evolving idea of 'man', the keystone of humanism itself. In extreme cases, incompatible registers coexist manically within the same utterance, as in one of the most extraordinary of neoplatonic allegories, the *Heroic Frenzies* of Florio's friend Giordano Bruno. In this sequence of sonnets, dedicated to the ideal courtier, soldier, scholar, Sir Philip Sidney, in which the poems, many of them on mythological subjects, are interspersed with interpretative dialogues, the language of Petrarchan idealisation decomposes before our eyes into a pathological horror and contempt:

> for those eyes, for those cheeks, for that breast, for that whiteness, for that vermilion, for that speech, for those teeth, for those lips, that hair, that dress, that robe, that glove, that slipper, that shoe, that reserve, that little smile, that wryness, that window-widow, that eclipsed sun, that scourge, that disgust, that stink, that tomb, that latrine, that menstruum, that carrion, that quartan ague, that excessive injury and distortion of nature, which with surface appearance, a shadow, a phantasm, a dream, a Circean enchantment put to the service of nature, deceives us as a species of beauty.
>
> (Bruno 1964: 60)

For the humanist, such contradictions can be both disabling and productive. The ironic reflexiveness and combative openness of humanist discourse can license the most disconcerting lurches from the serenely cerebral into what Mikhail Bakhtin calls the 'lower bodily stratum', the realm of the obscene, the disreputable, the grotesque, of raucous laughter and scatological irreverence. Erasmus' *Praise of Folly* is the ribald antitype of the *Utopia* of his friend More, whose name (*Moriae encomium*) it punningly appropriates; and the *Gargantua and Pantagruel* of François Rabelais unleashes a devastating onslaught of obscenity and visceral mockery against the patriarchs of ecclesiatical and intellectual authority.

In a different mode, the tensions of an aspiring masculinity torn between the active and the passionate, the soldier and the lover, can generate magnificent rhetorical and dramatic energy, as in the most reckless and eloquent of Elizabethan heroes, Marlowe's Tamburlaine the Great. Besieging Damascus, and about to engage in battle with the King of Arabia and his ally the Egyptian Sultan, this Mongolian superman pauses to reflect on the grief his inevitable victory will cause to the Sultan's daughter Zenocrate, with whom he is in love, and to ponder the strange, indefinable power of female beauty.

What is beauty, saith my sufferings, then?
If all the pens that ever poets held
Had fed the feeling of their masters' thoughts,
And every sweetness that inspir'd their hearts,
Their minds, and muses on admired themes;
If all the heavenly quintessence they still [distill]
From their immortal flowers of poesy,
Wherein, as in a mirror, we perceive
The highest reaches of a human wit;
If these had made one poem's period,
And all combin'd in beauty's worthiness,
Yet should there hover in their restless heads
One thought, one grace, one wonder, at the least,
Which into words no virtue can digest.

(Marlowe 1969: 167–68)

Unlike his author, Tamburlaine is not much of a reader, so we need not suspect him of whiling away his off-duty hours with a copy of Castiglione, who might almost have had his character and predicament in mind when he wrote that under the influence of beauty the courtier shall

be out of all bitterness and wretchedness that young men feel (in a manner) continually, as jealousies, suspicions, disdains, angers, desperations and certain rages full of madness ... He shall do no wrong to the husband, father, brethren or kinsfolk of the woman beloved.

(Castiglione 1928: 317)

But if the warrior is susceptible to the mysterious force of the feminine, he must also fear his own susceptibility as a dangerous weakness, which he struggles, in a passage of tortuously congested reasoning, to reconcile with the imperatives of manly virtue:

But how unseemly is it for my sex,
My discipline of arms and chivalry,
My nature, and the terror of my name,
To harbour thoughts effeminate and faint!
Save only that in beauty's just applause,

> With whose instinct the soul of man is touched,
> And every warrior that is rapt with love
> Of fame, of valour, and of victory,
> Must needs have beauty beat on his conceits:
> I thus conceiving, and subduing both,
> That which hath stoop'd the chiefest of the gods,
> Even from the fiery-spangled veil of heaven,
> To feel the lowly warmth of shepherds' flames,
> And march in cottages of strowed reeds,
> Shall give the world to note, for all my birth,
> That virtue solely is the sum of glory,
> And fashions men with true nobility.
>
> (Marlowe 1969: 168)

Of course Tamburlaine, described disarmingly in the list of characters as 'a Scythian shepherd', is no courtier, and in asserting an aggressive meritocracy of 'virtue' against the niceties of courtly rank he places himself outside the courtier's fastidious dilemmas of identity, and closer to the ruthless *virtù* of Machiavelli's Prince. A product of what Stephen Greenblatt (1980) calls 'self-fashioning', he owes nothing to social position or convention, and is thus free to redefine virtue as military conquest ('glory'); and if he can 'conceive' the power of love that reduced Zeus himself to the indignity of a shepherd's hovel, he can also 'subdue' it. The rhetorical virtuosity is impressive, but the strain shows in the clotted syntax and the hammering insistence on having it both ways, and the passage graphically transcribes the crisis of masculine identity that haunts the humanist project.

WIND FROM THE EAST

For his two great dramatic spectacles on the subject of Tamburlaine, Marlowe drew on popular accounts of the exploits of the Mongol chieftain Timur i Lenk (Timur the Lame), whose campaigns of invasion and conquest ranged from western China and northern India to Georgia, Armenia, Persia and the Holy Land. In 1401 his army captured and devastated Baghdad, the intellectual and cultural metropolis of Islam; and the following year he defeated the Ottoman sultan Bayezid I, so becoming – directly or through vassal princes – the master of a vast territory stretching from Delhi to Damascus and from the Black Sea to the Sahara. Timur, a devout if uncompromising Muslim, is said to have hesitated before attacking his fellow-believer Bayezid, and (untypically) to have treated him with respect after his capture. Marlowe's hero has no such misgivings. He humiliates his imperial captive, displaying him in a cage and goading him to a shameful suicide; and, taking his victory for proof that the God of the Qur'an, like his biblical counterpart, is a powerless imposter, he orders the burning of

> the Turkish Alcoran
> And all the heaps of superstitious books
> Found in the temple of that Mahomet,
> Whom I have thought a God.

The historical Timur, at heart a tribal warlord and adventurer, had neither the administrative means nor, perhaps, the political appetite to consolidate his conquests into an empire, still less to push them further towards the heartlands of Mediterranean and northern Europe. After defeating Bayezid he headed back to Samarkand to build mosques, harass his Ming and Moghul neighbours and, Lear-like, carve up his conquests to distribute between his sons (with predictably Lear-like results). If Marlowe, two centuries later, can still conjure from his exploits a figure of authentic menace and Machiavellian glamour, it is by playing on two more contemporary anxieties: of invasion by a barbarian horde from the East and of Islam, both brought into sharp focus by the recent Ottoman advance on Vienna, which had seen a Muslim army camped on the Danube and beating at the gates of western Christendom. Thomas More expressed the general apprehension of the Ottoman's 'mighty strength and power, his high malice and hatred, and his incomparable cruelty', in terms that might have been describing Marlowe's protagonist. Even without the menacing proximity of an imperial army noted for its cruelty and determination, Islam could be relied upon to excite associations at once alarming and farcical. The popular notion of Muslims as a menagerie of lunatics and voluptuaries worshipping the heretical ravings (and the toenail clippings) of an illiterate huckster ensured that no sober or informed understanding of Islamic life was likely to gain a hearing. And while the Papacy saw Islam, and the Ottomans especially, as a direct threat to its secular authority and a competitor in the pursuit of European and worldwide dominion, Protestants like Martin Luther denounced its 'heaps of superstitious books' as a mish-mash of heresy and idolatry, and called for a holy war against the Ottoman, the contemporary embodiment of the Antichrist fore-told in the Old Testament Book of Daniel and the Gospels.

The Ottoman emperor commanding the Turkish army at Vienna, a figure far better fitted to the Marlovian 'thirst of reign and sweetness of a crown' than the energetic but unimperial Timur, was Suleiman II, who, in addition to his official titles of Sultan, Khan and Padishah, had inherited from his ancestor Mehmet II, conqueror of Constantinople, the style of Kaisar-i-Rum (Emperor of Rome), thus signalling that he regarded himself as the legit-imate heir to the cultural no less than the military and political inheritance of the Roman Caesars. From the perspective of Paris, London or indeed Rome itself, the 'fall' of Constantinople, the city of the first Christian emperor Constantine and hence the ancient metropolis of Christendom, could be presented, for public consumption at least, as a catastrophe portending the overthrow of civilisation by a rabble of beturbaned baby-eating barbarians. The baby-eating barbarians themselves saw the matter rather differently. The twenty-one-year-old Mehmet, fluent in the classical languages alongside his native Turkish and Persian, consciously modelled himself on the character and achievements of Alexander the Great and the heroes of the *Iliad*, having studied Herodotus, Livy and Plutarch, the chroniclers of ancient empires, with his tutor, the antiquarian and humanist Cyriac of Ancona. In short, Mehmet was every bit as much a humanistic prince, a 'European', as any Borgia, Medici or Tudor.

A comparable sense of continuity extended to Islam itself, which Muslim intellectuals regarded as the continuation and completion of Judaeo-Christian civilisation, the final revelatory reunion by Jahweh-Allah, through the last of his prophets, of the far-wandering children of Abraham. Then, as later, Christians and Jews were viewed by most Muslims not as hateful infidels but as fellow 'People of the Book'; and western teachers, artists and administrators were encouraged to settle in the new capital and its tributary cities. (Among them was the Venetian painter Gentile Bellini, who spent a year in Constantinople in 1479–80 and painted the fine portrait of Mehmet II that now hangs in the National Gallery in London.) Beyond the military, clerical and bureaucratic elite, and in striking contrast to the coercive proselytising of later conquests, including the salvationist imperialism of the British empire and the botched, bloodstained 'crusade for democracy' of our own times, there was no attempt forcibly to convert non-Muslims or to impose a Qur'anic *shariah* on their daily lives. Mehmet's grandson Bayezid II sent ships to Spain to rescue the Andalusian Jews from the persecutions that followed the expulsion of the Moors in 1492. An *ahdnama* (edict) of 1463, issued by Mehmet himself after the annexation of Bosnia-Herzegovina, and once described as 'the oldest declaration of human rights in history', forbade any of his subjects to 'attack, insult or endanger [the Catholic Bosnians], either their life or their property or the property of their Church'. Suleiman offered a similar indemnity to the Christian and Jewish inhabitants of Jerusalem, recognising it as a city sacred to all three faiths.

ISLAMIC HUMANISM

Islam is as varied, as complex, as riven by sects and schisms as any other system of belief; but in broad terms, and for all the fulminations of Luther and other reforming divines, Sunni (i.e. traditional) Islam as practised throughout the Ottoman empire had a good deal in common with the proto-Protestantism emerging in the same period in central and northern Europe. Unlike the expansionist Shi'ism of their Persian neighbours, whose clerical hierarchies and apocalyptically cultish theology betray the influence of Christianity, Sunnis in the Ottoman ecumene practised a soberly Qur'anic religion that emphasised the primacy of secular social and familial obligation and enjoined a private discipline of reading, prayer, piety and good works, unmolested by an officious clergy, of a kind that Huss and Wycliff, Calvin and even the bellicose Luther himself might in other circumstances have recognised and approved. Indeed, in its undogmatic reading of the Qur'an and its neighbourly cohabitation with other Abrahamic religions, Ottoman Islam makes most Protestant churches look hidebound and intolerant. And like Protestantism, it enjoyed a sometimes prickly but generally productive relationship with secular rationality, in particular with the poetry and philosophy of Greek antiquity. Three centuries earlier, the Andalusian philosopher Abu'l-Walid Ibn Rushd (widely known by his Latinised name Averroës) had argued that the Holy Book must be read with the eye of imagination, as a figural not a literal text, and that if interpreted in that spirit its injunctions did not and should not be made to conflict with the truths of reason or the obligations of everyday morality. His manuscript commentaries on the writings of Plato and Aristotle stand at the head of a distinguished line of Islamic *falasifa* (philosophers) and humanists (*adib*) that includes the mathematician and astronomer Abu Rayhan al-Biruni, the Kazakh polymath Abu Nasr al-Farabi (Alfarabius), the Persian philosophers Abu Ali al-Husain Ibn Sina (Avicenna) and Abu Ya'qub al-Sijistani, and the Tunisian historian Abu Zayd Ibn-Khaldun. Like their European successors many centuries later, these Muslim *umanisti* were Hellenists, reading (in Greek) Empedocles and Epicurus as well as Plato and Aristotle, and regarding the Hellenic influence on Islamic intellectual culture (in Joel Kraemer's words) 'not as innovation but as a return to roots and renovation' (Kraemer 1986: 3). Like them too they were philologists, grounding their definition of humanity (*insaniyya*) in language: not the language of grammarians and pedants but the living public utterance of the marketplace and mosque, law court and academy. 'The principal part of humanism', wrote Abdullah Ibn al-Muqaffa, 'is eloquent discourse, and the principal part of eloquent discourse is acquired through learning'; while a century later al-Hasan ben Jahl urged his readers to

> learn to speak eloquently; for it is through speech that man is superior to all other animals; and the more eloquent you are in speaking, the more worthy you are of humanity.
>
> (Makdisi 1990: 95)

Aristotelean commonplaces, no doubt; but we must remember that these commonplaces were being enunciated seven hundred years before Erasmus and eight hundred before Jonson and Bacon, at a time when Aristotle's name was all but unknown, and his writings unread, in his native country, as in the rest of Europe; enunciated, furthermore, by devout Muslims in Tehran and Tunis, Isfahan, Seville, Mosul, Basra and above all Baghdad, intellectual capital of the Abbasid caliphate, with its famous library and university, a city described by a recent historian as 'a microcosm of the Islamic world, a rendezvous of scholars from far and wide, of diverse cultural and religious backgrounds', a cosmopolis 'permeated by a spirit of scepticism and secularism' (Kraemer 1986: vii). Here we find, across the full spectrum of the arts and sciences, a humanist epistemology worldly in its openness to new knowledge yet seemingly at ease, in spirit if not always in reality, with Qur'anic orthodoxy. For the *falasifa*, the accents of faith may differ from those of reason, but both lead to truth, and piety places no constraints upon the furthest explorations of intellect or the plenary realisation of humanity. Above all, both knowledge and justice, the discoveries of art and science and the precepts of ethical citizenship, are securely anchored in human reason, needing no other authority, whether from supernatural revelation or from the whims of a despot. In the words of al-Sijistani, the Persian neoplatonist who convened an informal academy of students and fellow-philosophers in tenth-century Baghdad: 'He who swims in our sea has no shore but himself.'

Ibn Rushd wrote in Arabic, for fellow Arabs and in the first instance for his patron the Caliph Abu Yaq'ub. That his writings, and through them the centuries-old tradition of Muslim humanist scholarship, found a European readership is due to the efforts of Arabic-speaking Jewish scholars in Spain and Provence such as Moshe ben Maimon (Maimonides) of Cordoba and Todros Todrosi of Arles, who translated them from Arabic into Hebrew and thence into Latin, in which language they made the mainstream of Greek philosophy accessible, at first in manuscript, later in print, to a European readership. Small wonder, in view of its uncompromising rationalism, that 'Averroism' was soon added to the list of dangerous heresies against the doctrines of the Church, attracting the anathema of the archbishops of Paris, London and Canterbury. But in stimulating a new interest in Greek philosophy, and – the vital contribution of Ibn Rushd and his predecessors – in asserting its essential unity or at least compatibility with the spirit of Abrahamic scripture, it laid the foundations and provided the materials for the civic and ethical humanism of quattrocento Italy.

And for its humanist aesthetics, too. For two hundred years, a Latin translation of Ibn Rushd's *Middle Commentary* on Aristotle, made in 1256 by Hermann Alemannus from Todrosi's Hebrew version, was virtually the only access readers had to Aristotle's *Poetics*, from which all later discussions of tragic drama take their cue. The printing of the Greek text of Aristotle's works by Aldus Manutius in the 1490s was of course a great achievement; but its immediate impact was small, and Hermann, first printed in 1481 and again in 1515, remained the principal source for most readers until the later nineteenth century. Even today when we speak of a *catastrophe* or *catharsis* (both words straight out of the *Poetics*) or debate the relevance of the 'unities' in drama or the novel, or call someone a 'political animal' (from the opening sentence of the *Politics*) or deplore extremes and extol the virtues of moderation (the main argument of the *Ethics*), we enter into a ghostly colloquy, a game of Chinese whispers in which the Muslim philosophers of medieval Farab, Baghdad, Isfahan and Cordoba speak to us of Plato and Aristotle in the voices and languages of Provençal Jews and German Latinists. Behind the soldier, scholar, courtier of the Renaissance city-state stands the figure of a twelfth-century Arab with the *Republic* in one hand and the *Qur'an* in the other.

HUMANIST READING

Ibn Rushd addresses his work to all readers 'who follow the way of speculation and are eager for a knowledge of the truth'. The humanist is a speaker, a teacher; but the ideal subject of the humanist's discourse is a reader. Indeed, the relation between the two is fully reciprocal, for the purpose of reading is not only to learn but also to return that learning to the vivid medium of speech, and so to make it, and the learner, humanly visible ('Speak, that I may see thee'). Here again Florio is helpful, this time in his earlier primer for language learners, the *First Frutes* of 1587:

> By reading, many things are learned, who will have good counsel, let him read, who will see, and hear strange things, let him read: by reading, we have good forwarning, by reading, we learn to know the good from the bad, virtue from vice, & as the bee takes from one herb gum, from another wax, & from another honey, so by reading divers books, divers things are learned ... By reading we learn to be eloquent, and being eloquent, many and innumerable be the commodities that ensue of it; Eloquence hath force to make the coward couragious, the tyrant courteous & merciful: Eloquence persuadeth the good, dissuadeth the bad, comforteth the afflicted, banisheth fear from the fearful, pacifieth the insolent, and, as Cicero saith, vanquisheth cities, kingdoms, & castles with her force.
>
> (Florio 1587: 52, 57)

Eloquence, in short, is the mother of Utopia, distributing 'commodities', banishing fear and ambition, pacifying kingdoms; and the mother of eloquence is reading. If speaking makes us visible, reading teaches us to speak. It is noticeable how popular the figure of the reader, especially the woman reading, becomes in domestic portraiture from the later sixteenth century, from the richly dressed 'Woman reading a book', lost in pious or romantic reverie, in the Rosenwald *Book of Hours* (1533) to the women absorbed in books or letters so intimately painted by seventeenth-century Flemish artists such as Rembrandt, Gerrit Dou, Jan Vermeer and Pieter de Hooch. Unlike the formal portrait, there is in all these pictures a striking absence of 'pose', self-conscious, outer-directed. The painter is absent; and the spectator is a privileged, invisible witness, an involuntary voyeur, of a moment of pure inwardness. The reader, in silent colloquy with an unseen interlocutor, becomes the focal site of a new interiority.

What those readers in their speaking silences remind us is that at the centre of humanist activity is the book. All its values, its virtue and eloquence, its recklessness and moderation, its piety and obscenity, are textualised: grounded in books, taught through books, rehearsed, elaborated and disputed in books. A book, for the humanist, is a living thing; and a living thing is nothing other than an animated book. When Milton in *Areopagitica* (1644) calls a good book 'the precious lifeblood of a master spirit' (Milton 1990: 578), he only reciprocates what he had written a couple of years before, that 'he who would not be frustrate of his hope to write well hereafter in laudable things, ought himselfe to bee a true Poem, that is a composition, and patterne of the best and honourablest things' (Milton 1953: 57). And that *'master* spirit' indicates that, although so many of those painted readers, like so many of the subjects and addressees of humanist discourse, are women, and the activity of reading (*la lettura*) is feminised, the discourse itself is a manly one, a discipline of mastery. A large amount, perhaps the bulk, of humanist reading matter is concerned either with the acquisition and maintenance of political and social authority (*The Prince*, *The Courtier*, Thomas Elyot's *Boke named the Governour* (1531), Milton's *Of Education* (1644)) or, as Lorna Hutson has shown, with the masculine 'husbandry' of the conjugal and paternal household (Hutson 1994). As so often throughout the subsequent history of the word, the decisive semantic stress (hu*man*ism) falls on the second syllable; and never more so than when it lays claim to an encompassing universality.

PICO DELLA MIRANDOLA AND 'RENAISSANCE HUMANISM'

It is worth repeating, though, that to talk about 'humanism' in this context, in whatever incarnation – the Islamic humanism of the *falasifa*, the early Florentine or 'civic' humanism of Petrarch, Coluccio Salutati and Leonardo Bruni, the northern European Christian humanism of Erasmus and More, 'Latin' and 'Greek' humanisms – is a historical solecism. All are later constructions, not wrong for that reason but grouped and periodised into tidy narratives whose logic may tell us more about the concerns of those who compose them than about the writings they compose them from. So when, for example, three of the most eminent and learned historians of the period assert confidently that during the Italian Renaissance the term 'humanism' denoted primarily 'a specific intellectual program' and only incidentally suggested the more general set of values which have in recent times come to be called 'humanistic' (Cassirer 1948: 2–3), it takes a fair bit of nerve to disagree; but it needs to be said that all statements of that kind are seriously misleading. The term 'humanism' denoted nothing in the fifteenth and sixteenth centuries, in Italy or anywhere else, for the reason that no such term existed. Nor, except in the most hopelessly generalised sense, was there any 'specific intellectual program' for it to denote, if it had existed. True, there was an informal curriculum, the *studia humanitatis* or 'study of humanity', grounded in the reading of ancient Greek and Roman authors and the application of Platonic, Aristotelean and Ciceronian ideas and values to contemporary life; and the people who taught it or wrote about it sometimes referred to themselves as *umanisti* or 'humanists', a purely functional term that conferred no particular prestige. But if that adds up to an 'intellectual program', it is one characterised by a notable absence of coherence and a remarkable degree of discord. While Petrarch and his pupil Leonardo Bruni venerated Cicero as the supreme arbiter of public conduct and private virtue, the Byzantine philosopher Joannes Argyropoulos dismissed him as a bore and a dilettante. 'Platonic' humanists like Marsilio Ficino scorned the work of their 'Aristotelean' colleagues. The Catholic humanist More paid with his life for his devotion to a Church for which his friend Erasmus had little but contempt. And if these intellectual divergences can be seen as examples of the benign *coincidentia oppositorum* or harmonious opposition of which the humanists were so fond, it has to be said that more often than not they were expressed with an aggressively personal offensiveness that scuttles any notion of companionable collegiality. So radical and uncompromising, indeed, are the differences separating one 'humanist' from another that you begin to wonder whether that word too has any useful meaning; and it is noticeable, in fact, that historians of the period disagree quite sharply about whether some of the key figures, such as Petrarch, More, da Vinci, Luther or Calvin, can be called humanists at all.

A vivid example of the problems of humanist historiography is the case of the Florentine nobleman Giovanni Pico della Mirandola, author of a Latin oration 'On the Dignity of Man' which has been called 'the manifesto of Renaissance humanism' (Craven 1981). In fact the Oration, intended to serve as a preface to a set of nine hundred contentious theological theses and not printed in Pico's lifetime, was not given the title by which it is generally known until some seventy years later. It consists largely of a defence, florid in style and astonishingly eclectic in its variety of literary and mythological reference, of the elevated calling of the philosopher, a debate of some importance in fifteenth-century Florence, where the rival claims of the active and the contemplative life articulated some of the central themes at issue in the political transition from citizen republic to Medicean principality and the relations between the independent city-state and the Roman Church.

But the Oration's fame, and its extraordinary prominence in later accounts of humanism, derive from the first few pages, in which the biblical Creator of Genesis announces to the newly formed Adam that he will stand apart from the rest of creation by virtue of the special freedom and versatility with which he has been endowed. Whereas all other creatures are circumscribed by the natural disposition conferred upon them, Man alone has the capacity to choose his own nature.

> He therefore took man as a creature of indeterminate nature and, assigning him a place in the middle of the world, addressed him thus: 'Neither a fixed abode nor a form that is thine alone nor any function peculiar to thyself have we given thee, Adam, to the end that according to thy longing and according to thy judgment thou mayest have and possess what abode, what form, and what functions thou thyself shalt desire. The nature of all other beings is limited and constrained within the bounds of laws prescribed by Us. Thou, constrained by no limits, in accordance with thine own free will, in whose hand We have placed thee, shalt ordain for thyself the limits of thy nature. We have set thee at the world's centre that thou mayest from thence more easily observe whatever is in the world. We have made thee neither of heaven nor of earth, neither mortal nor immortal, so that with freedom of choice and with honour, as though the maker and moulder of thyself, thou mayest fashion thyself in whatever shape thou shalt prefer.'

(Cassirer 1948: 224)

This unique freedom, Adam is told, can be used 'to degenerate into the lower forms of life' or 'to be reborn into the higher forms', allegorised by Pico as the three highest orders in the Dionysian hierarchy of angels, which are taken in turn as a figure for the three-part choice of life that structures so much humanist thinking.

> Let us consider what they do, what sort of life they lead. If we also come to lead that life (for we have the power), we shall then equal their good fortune. The Seraph burns with the fire of love. The Cherub glows with the splendour of intelligence. The Throne stands by the steadfastness of judgment. Therefore if, in giving ourselves over to the active life, we have after due consideration undertaken the care of the lower beings, we shall be strengthened with the firm stability of Thrones. If, unoccupied by deeds, we pass our time in the leisure of contemplation, considering the Creator in the creature and the creature in the Creator, we shall be all ablaze with Cherubic light. If we long with love for the Creator himself alone, we shall speedily flame up with His consuming fire into a Seraphic likeness.
>
> (Cassirer 1948: 227)

The first part of the Oration, which J.A. Symonds called 'the Epiphany of the modern spirit', certainly reads, for all its abstruse neoplatonic allegorising and its exotic syncretism of Jewish and Christian with Greco-Roman, Zoroastrian, Chaldean and Arabic philosophies, like an eloquent exposition of many of the themes elaborated by Burckhardt and his successors: the dignity and freedom of man, individualism, wide intellectual curiosity and a refusal to submit to the constraints of clerical orthodoxy. Furthermore, Pico's rank, as Count of Mirandola, and his lordly contempt for convention and mediocrity, seemed to suit him for the role of courtier in the Castiglione mould, while the fact that the Church suppressed his nine hundred theses as heretical and refused to allow him to dispute them publicly, as he wished, enhanced his glamour as a heroic pioneer of free-thinking modernity.

In the same spirit, its influence has been detected throughout the writing of the following two centuries, confirming its status as a seminal text. When Marlowe's Tamburlaine, discoursing philosophically of

> Our souls, whose faculties can comprehend
> The wondrous architecture of the world,
> And measure every wandering planet's course,
> Still climbing after knowledge infinite,
> And always moving as the restless spheres,
>
> (Marlowe 1969: 133)

adds the contemplative 'splendour of intelligence' to the active 'steadfastness of judgment' he has already shown as a victorious general, he seems to stand self-created as a philosopher-prince of Mirandolan lineage. The older brother in Milton's Ludlow masque *Comus* (1634) reassures his younger sibling with an account of the protean capacities of human freedom that is at the same time a defence of the effective power of 'divine philosophy' (Milton 1990: 75–76), while the later *Paradise Lost*, with its syncretic diversity of reference, its angelic hierarchs instructing an unfallen Adam in the responsibilities of free will and its determination to penetrate the mystery of 'Things unattempted yet in Prose or Rime' (Milton 1990: 150), looks like the realisation, almost two hundred years later, of Pico's unconsummated project. Most frequently, perhaps, the Oration has been seen as the direct inspiration behind one of the most commonly quoted passages in Shakespeare, Hamlet's

> What a piece of work is a man! How noble in reason! how infinite in faculty! in form, in moving, how express and admirable! in action how like an angel! in apprehension how like a god! the beauty of the world! the paragon of animals!
>
> (*Hamlet*, II, ii)

Actually, 'most commonly misquoted' might have been better, since the first words are usually rendered as 'What a piece of work is Man'. This is how the sentence is almost always remembered conversationally, and it is often encountered in this form in print, even finding its way into a recent history of humanism by a distinguished historian of the subject (Bullock 1985: 44).

To point this out is not a piece of cheap pedantry. The apparently trivial omission of the indefinite article decisively shifts the sense, in a way that may throw light on the significance attributed by Burckhardt, Symonds and others to the Oration itself. It has already been noted that the title 'On the Dignity of Man', which so decisively predisposes the meaning and purpose of the Oration, was not given to it by Pico himself. His nephew Gianfrancesco, printing it for the first time in 1496, called it simply *Oratio quaedam elegantissima* ('a certain very stylish discourse'), and it was not until Frobenius' Basle edition of 1557 that it received the Latin title by which it has since been known. The phrase 'dignity of man' does not occur in the text itself, and it is striking how little interest Pico shows, after the opening allegorical flourish of God's apostrophe to Adam, in defining the properties of a generic entity called 'Man'. In Latin, in any case, the distinction between 'a man' (any), 'the man' (particular) and 'man' (universal) is grammatically indifferent, since the language lacks both definite and indefinite articles: the Basle title, *De hominis dignitate*, could as easily be translated 'On a man's worthiness'. The usual version, with its portentous evocation of a transcendent 'Man', belongs, like so much else of Renaissance 'humanism', not to the fifteenth century but to the nineteenth. Pico's 'very stylish discourse' was not fully translated into English until 1944, and Symonds seems to have been the first, in 1882, to give it its English title.

If Hamlet's elusive little 'a' opens up some of the problems of reading the Oration, with Burckhardt, Symonds, Cassirer and many others, as the founding document of a later universalising humanism, his sardonic repudiation of his own humanist 'piece of work' (the phrase means 'masterpiece') exposes some of the other issues obscured by the rhetorical figure of universal Man.

> And yet, to me, what is this quintessence of dust? man delights not me;
> no, nor woman neither, though, by your smiling, you seem to say so.
> (*Hamlet*, II, ii)

Shifting adroitly between two modalities of 'man' ('humanity' and 'male person'), Hamlet exposes the extent to which, unlike later humanisms, the writing of fifteenth-, sixteenth- and seventeenth-century humanists is explicitly and self-consciously entangled in the problematics of sexual difference. Machiavelli's or Ficino's masculine *virtù*, for ever on its guard against the blandishments and treacheries of female Fortune; Erasmus' sluttish Folly vaunting her female ancestry and reproductive potency, and laughing coarsely at the pretensions of male philosophers and prelates; Bruno's philosophical Actaeon destroyed by his own glimpse of virginal wisdom; Spenser's manly Guyon laying waste with puritanical relish the seductive allurements of Acrasia and her garden of earthly delights: at every point, the humanist imagination is haunted by sexual terror and desire (Bruno 1964: 123; Spenser 1912: 139). As Florio shows, its very language is sexually saturated, and it would be virtually impossible, and almost certainly futile, to disentangle its allegorical figurations from the ideological commitments that they articulate. When Francis Bacon calls science *temporis partus masculus* ('the male progeny of time'), or Milton writes that 'Laws are Masculin Births', the metaphor of male parthenogenesis adumbrates a regime of knowledge and power, set out more explicitly in the former's *New Atlantis* and the latter's *Tenure of Kings and Magistrates*, in which women, quite literally, do not figure (Bacon 1905: 710–32; Milton 1971: 32).

Far from the evasively ungendered 'universality' of Comtean humanity, the 'man' of the early humanists is an embattled and uncertain construction (a 'piece of work', indeed), his aspirations to the generic inclusiveness of the human foundering on the inescapable limitations of the masculine. All Pico's eloquence cannot disguise the oddity of his opening *mythus*, an Adamic Paradise without an Eve. If his paean to the metamorphic creativity of contemplative intellect anticipates the chaste rapture of Andrew Marvell's 'Garden', in whose green shade

> The mind, that ocean where each kind
> Does straight its own resemblance find;
> Yet it creates, transcending these,
> Far other worlds, and other seas,

> (lines 43–46)

it too collapses, like the poem, into a bathetic misogyny that reveals yet again the remorseless absurdity of would-be ungendered 'man':

> Such was that happy garden-state,
> While man there walked without a mate ...
> But 'twas beyond a mortal's share
> To wander solitary there:
> Two paradises 'twere in one
> To live in paradise alone.

(lines 57–64)

Marvell's witty explicitness is as refreshing as it is unusual. In Pico's case, the problematics of gender are ruthlessly suppressed in his argument, with its all-male cast of angels and patriarchal authorities, from Moses and Zoroaster to Plato and Paul, only to resurface, yet again, in his language:

> For if you see one abandoned to his appetites crawling on the ground, it is a plant and not a man you see; if you see one blinded by the vain illusions of imagery, as it were of Calypso, and, softened by their gnawing allurement, delivered over to his senses, it is a beast and not a man you see.

(Cassirer 1948: 226)

And as so often in humanist writing, the crude misogyny which identifies the female, in this case the Homeric sorceress Calypso (step-sister to Bruno's 'Circean enchantment'), with the bestiality of desire coexists without discomfort, the positive and negative poles of humanist patriarchy, with a rapt idealism that approvingly feminises the contemplative act itself. Purified by philosophy, the soul (Latin *anima*, grammatically feminine)

> shall herself be made the house of God, and to the end that as soon as she has cast out her uncleanness through moral philosophy and dialectic, adorned herself with manifold philosophy as with the splendour of a courtier, and crowned the pediments of her doors with the garlands of theology, the King of Glory may descend and, coming with his Father, make his stay with her. If she show herself worthy of so great a guest, she shall, by the boundless mercy which is his, in golden raiment like a wedding gown, and surrounded

by a varied throng of sciences, receive her beautiful guest not
merely as a guest but as a spouse from whom she will never be parted.

(Cassirer 1948: 232)

In the century since Symonds, Pater and Arnold wrote, one or
two dissenting voices have been raised, pointing to the rhetorical
and functional character of the Oration, the incoherence and
conventionality of many of its ideas, the 'extravagance and pos-
turing' of its claims for philosophy, its unrepresentativeness both
of Pico's writings and of humanist thought in general (see Craven
1981). But these are minority views. The Burckhardtian reading
remains the dominant one, underpinning the proto-modernity of
the Renaissance and its unbroken continuity with the present.
Giving for the first time 'a positive method and dignity' to the
'haphazard and superficial' speculations of the humanists, the
Oration 'summarizes with grand simplicity and in pregnant form
the whole intent of the Renaissance and its entire concept of
knowledge' (Cassirer 1948: 222), thus inaugurating a 'humanistic religion' which

signifies the beginning of the evolution which, via the Enlightenment,
finds its most consistent continuation in what in recent years has
been called 'Humanism'.

(Gelder 1964: 7–8)

Against all this, it becomes necessary to restate the real subject of
Pico's eloquence: not 'the dignity of man', which is no more than
an allegorical and rhetorical gambit, but the absolute compatibility and hence universality of all known investigations into
'the causes of things, the ways of nature, the plan of the universe,
the purposes of God, and the mysteries of heaven and earth'
(Cassirer 1948: 237–38). In this extraordinary enterprise, which
takes to new lengths the 'syncretic' or synthesising passion of
Platonic humanism, Hebrew and Chaldee sages jostle amicably
with Pythagoras and Aristotle, the Decalogue and Gospels keep
company with Orphic and Hermetic mysteries, natural magic
and numerology, medieval churchmen like Scotus and Aquinas
rub shoulders with Arab philosophers like Ibn Sina and Ibn

Rushd, and all are cheerfully embraced within the generous doctrinal bosom of the Mother Church in Rome.

This shows a degree of political optimism, certainly (his enemies called it arrogance); and it is something of a tribute to the humanistic broad-mindedness of the Church that, although Pico's offer of a public disputation was declined, only thirteen of the nine hundred theses were thought theologically objectionable by the papal commission appointed to examine them. But it also suggests that, in spite of his publicly expressed contempt in his *Apologia* for their intellectual inadequacies, the Curial authorities hardly saw the theses as the work of a dangerous theological modernist, an Italian Luther or Calvin. Unorthodox as they were, most of the issues raised had been the subject of theological dispute for centuries, and the commission pointed to the truly heterodox nature of Pico's project when it condemned him not for innovation but for 'reviving several of the errors of gentile philosophers which are already disproved and obsolete' (Craven 1981: 47ff.).

I have spent some time on the Oration and its author as a way of showing how strong even now is the hold of the Burckhardtian narrative of the Renaissance as the cradle of modernity, and of the humanists as the fearless cosmonauts of the future. In this view, the 'Man' of Mirandolan humanism is not, as Michel Foucault put it, 'an invention of recent date ... perhaps nearing its end', simply one among the many historical objects of human knowledge, but a still-unrealised *telos*, a terminal truth towards which human reason has been striving, through the infested swamps and enchanted forests of dogma and superstition, since the dawn of history itself. Three historical tropes structure the myth and give it its seductive coherence: the *break with the past* (the *Encyclopaedia Britannica* (1993) entry on the Renaissance describes it as 'a complete break ... with medieval culture'); the *return to the source* (the same article defines humanism as 'a return to the Hellenic sources of Western culture'), and *unbroken continuity with the present*. And like all adventure stories, this one has its heroes (Petrarch, Pico, Michelangelo) and its villains (the Church, Islam, the 'Middle Ages'), which perhaps helps to explain its obdurate hold on the historiographic imagination.

But while its ideological grip persists, its explanatory power is negligible. The humanists never did propose what Lisa Jardine calls 'a logic of discovery' (Jardine 1974: 14). If they used the word at all, it was only in the older sense of *re*-covery, the disclosure of things already known, though sometimes forgotten. Their beloved 'dialectic' was not the dynamically forward-driving force of Hegel and Marx but a method of teaching, where possible from the ancient texts, things already written, and of discussing them in a language inspired by the eloquence and *umanità* of the ancients. To bring this out clearly, it will be useful to compare Pico with another writer who, a century later, set out to explore what the Oration calls 'the causes of things, the ways of nature, the plan of the universe, the purposes of God, and the mysteries of heaven and earth' (Cassirer 1948: 237–38).

4

HUMANISM AND ENLIGHTENMENT

Why should we not introduce man into our work, as he has been placed in the universe? Why not make man the central focus?

(Denis Diderot)

NATURE AND SCIENCE

In a famous passage in the *Great Instauration* (1620) that intriguingly anticipates Nietzsche's 'four errors', Francis Bacon describes the four 'Idols and false notions which are now in possession of the human understanding', and which prevent human beings from arriving at a clear understanding of the world in which they live. First, he writes, are the 'Idols of the Tribe', so called because they 'have their foundation in human nature itself, and in the tribe or race of men'. They are responsible for an innate tendency to attribute human significance to natural phenomena, populating the universe with human intelligence and desire, from the anthropoid totems of traditional religion to the casual poetry of 'raging tempests'. Second are the 'Idols of the Cave' that govern individual temperament, predisposing each of us to find particular patterns of significance in the contingency of things; for 'every one ... has a cave or den of his own, which refracts and discolours the light of nature'. Third are the linguistic confusions that result from the attempt to describe and classify things using ready-made vocabularies and concepts, which Bacon calls the 'Idols of the Market Place', 'on account of the commerce and consort of men there'; since 'it is by discourse that men associate; and words are imposed according to the apprehension of the vulgar'. Finally, there are the 'Idols of the Theatre', the theoretical systems and explanatory narratives 'which have immigrated into men's minds from the various dogmas of philosophies', so called 'because in my judgement all the received systems are but so many stage-plays, representing worlds of their own creation after an unreal and scenic fashion', into which every fragment of experience, however awkward or contradictory, must be made to fit (Bacon 1905: 263–64).

Bacon has often been claimed as a humanist. Like Erasmus, he despised the formalism and traditionalism of the ancient universities. His *Essays*, addressed like so much humanist didactic to a young nobleman, are a primer of civic *umanità* such as might have been written by Ascham or Elyot. For him, as for Machiavelli, the measure of all knowledge must be not its theoretical consistency or conformity to some ancient authority, but its practical usefulness and reliability; and he would certainly have relished the iconoclastic *chutzpah* of the French humanist Pierre de la Ramée (Peter Ramus), who earned his doctorate from the University of Paris by defending the thesis that 'all the things that Aristotle taught were fictions [*commentitia*]'. Bacon's ambition, expressed through the experimental philosophers of his utopian *New Atlantis*, was to open a way, through the accumulated Idols of error, habit and prejudice, to 'the Knowledge of Causes, and Secrett Motions of Things; And the Enlarging of the bounds of Humane Empire, to the Effecting of all Things possible' (Bacon 1974: 239), a project that recalls Pico's desire to penetrate 'the causes of things, the ways of nature, the plan of the universe, the purposes of God, and the mysteries of heaven and earth'.

The truth is, however, that under the pitiless gaze of Baconian empiricism the pretensions of the humanists wither. Bacon thinks of knowledge not, like Pico, as contemplative wisdom but as 'empire', active conquest for practical ends. 'What men want to learn from nature', writes Adorno in *The Dialectic of Enlightenment*, 'is how to use it in order wholly to dominate it and men' (Adorno 1973: 9). The human-centred world of humanist anthropology, with its elaborate correspondences of human and cosmic and its assurance that, in the words of Plato's Protagoras, 'man is the measure of all things', is exposed as no more than a tribal *folie de grandeur*. And whereas for the humanists language, Hamlet's 'discourse of reason', not only unlocks the mysteries of the cosmos but is itself numbered among them, Bacon, in a coolly revisionary reading of one of those mythological narratives in which the humanists found an image of the amorous identity of the natural and the human, asserts an absolute separation between the primary objectivity and self-sufficiency of nature and the secondary order of language through which it is labelled and classified:

> it is no marvel if no loves are attributed to Pan, besides his marriage with Echo. For the world enjoys itself, and in itself all things that are ... The world therefore can have no loves, nor any want (being content with itself), unless it be of discourse. Such is the nymph Echo, a thing not substantial but only a voice ... for that is the true philosophy which echoes most faithfully the voices of the world itself, and is written as it were at the world's own dictation; being nothing else than the image and reflexion thereof, to which it adds nothing of its own, but only iterates and gives it back.

> (Bacon 1905: 516–18)

To the humanists, these metamorphic myths, like language (*mythos* means 'speech'), resemble a world which is itself a book, an incarnate speech act. Words and things share a common nature, and the imagination is permitted a glimpse of the virginal truths of reason. Bacon's language too is saturated with erotic metaphor, charging the pursuit of knowledge with associations of seduction and sexual conquest. But unlike the despised Aristoteleans, whose ⁀eble abstractions can only 'catch and grasp' at knowledge, leaving 'Nature herself untouched and inviolate', Bacon sets out to 'seize or detain her', compelling her into a 'chaste, holy and legal wedlock' from which the fruits of science will issue (ibid.: 12–13). This is itself a powerful myth: Genevieve Lloyd calls it 'Bacon's main contribution to our ways of thinking about mind's relation to the rest of Nature' (Lloyd 1993: 13). But his use of the story of Pan and Echo, by contrast, is purely illustrative and tactical. Nature, serenely self-absorbed, has no need of speech. Language, contemplating it from afar with a yearning that can never be consummated, is condemned to iteration and reflection.

At the same time, the Baconian challenge to (and for) intellectual authority goes far beyond the sceptical anti-Aristoteleanism of Ramus and the Florentine Platonists, the humanist inclination to treat the golden codgers of antiquity as 'guides, not commanders' (Jonson 1975: 379). If humanist dialectic, as Lisa Jardine has argued, is essentially conservative, the eloquent exposition of a body of already existing knowledge 'within a textbook tradition', Bacon by contrast offers a radical 'logic of discovery' (Jardine 1974: 17), a methodological will to power that threatens to dissolve all intellectual authority in its unappeasable hunger for empire:

> And therefore it is fit that I publish and set forth those conjectures of mine which make hope in this matter reasonable; just as Columbus did, before that wonderful voyage of his across the Atlantic, when he gave the reasons for his conviction that new lands and continents might be discovered besides those which were known before; which reasons, though rejected at first, were afterwards made good by experience, and were the causes and beginnings of great events.
>
> (Bacon 1905: 287)

In this sense Bacon, or rather the 'Baconianism' that in the course of the seventeenth century was to find its concrete realisation in the materialist sociology of Thomas Hobbes and the systematic empiricism of the Royal Society, marks the historical terminus of 'Renaissance humanism'; or rather *one* of its historical termini. For if there is a paradox in the humanist Bacon serving notice of redundancy on the humanist enterprise, it is certainly no sharper than the poignancy of the even more deeply humanist

Jean Calvin devising for his Genevan congregation a theocracy as absolute, and as securely grounded in secular power, as any medieval Pope could have dreamt of. In England, whose Calvinist national church was established and governed by the scholarly Latinist Elizabeth Tudor, herself a pupil of the humanist Roger Ascham, Protestant intellectuals continued through the later sixteenth and early seventeenth centuries to cultivate their humanist gardens, but only at the cost of ignoring the contradictions, always latent within the volatile compound of 'Christian humanism', between Calvin's all-powerful, all-knowing deity, in whose mind every sinful human destiny awaits its preordained comeuppance, and the humanist dream of self-determination; contradictions that make themselves felt everywhere in the writings of Protestant humanists like Philip Sidney, Edmund Spenser, Christopher Marlowe, John Donne and John Milton.

HUMANISM AND RELIGION

Each of those, and many others, could provide material for a chapter. The 'bate' or conflict that the protagonist of Sidney's sonnet-sequence *Astrophil and Stella* feels between his 'will', his shameful desire for the unattainable Stella, and his 'wit', his intellectual and moral understanding, echoes the painful paradoxes of the same writer's *Apology for Poetry*, in which poetry torments the 'erected wit' of the aspiring humanist with glimpses of a distant perfection from which the 'infected will' is forever exiled (Sidney 1965: 101). For the wealthy and cosmopolitan Sidney, who seemed to some contemporaries the embodiment of Castiglionean courtliness, these antinomies may have been a clever game, though the writing hints otherwise. In Spenser, materially dependent and thus ideologically constrained in ways unnecessary for his patrician friend and patron, the effort to reconcile a Calvinist sense of worthlessness with a humanist commitment to classical beauty and eloquence troubles the writing with a profound unease, and there are few things in the poetry of the period as revealing as the passage in the second book of his ruined allegorical epic *The Faerie Queene* in which the idyllically hedonistic Bower of Bliss, whose iridescent detail testifies to the breadth of Spenser's reading in the canon of humanist pleasure, is laid waste, in a frenzy of grim self-mortification, by the Calvinist hero Sir Guyon, who only moments before was himself on the point of falling under its spell.

> But all those pleasant bowres and Pallace braue,
>   Guyon broke downe, with rigour pittilesse;
>   Ne ought their goodly workmanship might saue
>   Them from the tempest of his wrathfulnesse,
>   But that their blisse he turn'd to balefulnesse:
>   Their groues he feld, their gardins did deface,
>   Their arbers spoyle, their Cabinets suppresse,
>   Their banket houses burne, their buildings race,
> And of the fairest late, now made the fowlest place ...

> Said Guyon, See the mind of beastly man,
>   That hath so soon forgot the excellence
>   Of his creation, when he life began.
>
> (Spenser 1912: 139)

Torn between *voluptas* and *pietas*, pleasure and piety, the poem releases the guilty tensions in an explosion of self-justifying violence. But Guyon is too obviously an allegory, a convenient fiction. He lacks the complexity, the unexpectedness, of the real. From the humorous folktales and comic-strip escapades of the German *Faustbuch*, Spenser's younger contemporary Marlowe was able to conjure a narrative that articulates in its central figure the tortured contradictions of Calvinist humanism, and to animate them with a tragic eloquence. Driven by a humanist will to knowledge and a Mirandolan sense of limitless potential, tormented by a conviction of his own worthlessness and inexorable damnation, Faustus swings uncontrollably between the hostile poles of knowledge and belief. A syncretic Hellenism ('I confound Hell in Elysium', he assures Mephostophilis, who presumably knows otherwise) alternates vertiginously with Calvinist despair ('Now hast thou but one bare hour to live / And then thou must be damned perpetually') (Marlowe 1969: 336). 'Have not I made blind Homer sing to me?', he comforts himself in his terminal wretchedness, a doomed Petrarch communing with the ancients (ibid.: 285). But the Homeric Helen who consoles him in the shadow of his final hour is no vision of unsurpassable Greek loveliness; she is a succubus, a fraud, a mocking diabolical hologram.

Marlowe's play has a provocative and unsettling ambivalence that the political functionary Spenser could not afford. Faustus' devilish contract, his contemptuous dismissal of the entire curriculum of orthodox knowledge and belief in favour of necromancy, his blasphemous assertion that 'A sound magician is a demi-god' (Marlowe 1969: 268), are neither endorsed nor condemned – or rather, they seem to be *both* endorsed and condemned. Humanist aspiration and, in Mephostophilis, the desolation of the damned are voiced with equal vividness. Magic, in which Faustus believes he has found a logic of discovery that will truly unlock the Baconian 'knowledge of causes, and secret motions of things' and admit him to 'the enlarging of the bounds of human empire, to the effecting of all things possible', is exposed as a sham. Mephostophilis is not 'conjured' by the scholar's imprecations, he comes unbidden, drawn by the smell of damnation; and the causes and secret motions of the universe elude the hero, who dwindles from a fearless cosmonaut of the intellect back into the harmless prankster of the *Faustbuch*. At the same time, the religious orthodoxy that condemns him for venturing 'more than heavenly power permits' seems both empty and laughable, a lumbering masquerade of deadly sins and capering demons. Like the enigmatic *dieu caché* of the Jansenists, the Calvinist deity remains hidden, perhaps indifferent (Goldmann 1964).

There is a Faustian confrontation at the climax of the last and perhaps the least-read of Milton's significant poems, *Paradise Regained* (1671). A young man is led by an older one to the summit of a mountain, from which opens out a panoramic prospect of the Mediterranean world. What his companion shows him is, in effect, a humanist epiphany of origins: a living encounter with the ancients, in a scene bathed in the lambent glow of nostalgic longing:

> behold
> Where on the Aegean shore a city stands,
> Built nobly, pure the air and light the soil –

> Athens, the eye of Greece, mother of arts
> And eloquence, native to famous wits
> Or hospitable, in her sweet recess,
> City or suburban, studious walks and shades;
> See there the olive-grove of Academe,
> Plato's retirement, where the Attic bird
> Trills her thick-warbled notes the summer long;
> There, flowery hill, Hymettus, with the sound
> Of bees' industrious murmur, oft invites
> To studious musing; there Ilissus rolls
> His whispering stream; within the walls then view
> The schools of ancient sages – his who bred
> Great Alexander to subdue the world,
> Lyceum there; and painted Stoa next:
> There thou shalt hear and learn the secret power
> Of harmony, in tones and numbers hit
> By voice or hand, and various-measured verse,
> Ælian charms and Dorian lyric odes,
> And his who gave them breath, but higher sung,
> Blind Melesigenes, thence Homer called,
> Whose poem Phœbus challenged for his own.

(Milton 1990: 492–93)

This evocation by a blind poet of an Athens he had been unable, even when younger and still sighted, to visit (a projected trip to Greece over thirty years earlier had been cut short at Rome) is a compelling testimony to the hallucinatory power of the humanist imagination, not least in its habit of seeing everything, as Johnson said of Milton, 'through the spectacles of books' (Johnson 1906: 128). For the description of the city and its environs is exclusively literary, and owes nothing to an indulgent topographic nostalgia. The 'flowery hill, Hymettus' and the little river Ilissus that rises on its lower slopes are there for their Platonic associations, and even the Attic nightingales that sing among the olives of the Academy and neighbouring Colonus owe their tuneful presence to Sophocles, not ornithology.

In context, however, this set piece of humanist reverie is powerfully dramatised, and ironised. For the elderly Hellenist is the Devil, and his companion, to whom he is offering all that wisdom, power and beauty in return for a very reasonable Faustian concession ('On this condition, if thou wilt fall down / And worship me as thy superior Lord'), is the youthful Jesus, whose reply demolishes with casual brutality three centuries of humanist scholarship, and much of Milton's own writing into the bargain.

> But these are false, or little else but dreams,
> Conjectures, fancies, built on nothing firm . . .
>   . . .Who, therefore, seeks in these
> True wisdom finds her not, or, by delusion
> Far worse, her false resemblance only meets,
> An empty cloud. However, many books,
> Wise men have said, are wearisome; who reads
> Incessantly, and to his reading brings not
> A spirit or judgement equal or superior,
> (And what he brings, what needs he elsewhere seek?)
> Uncertain and unsettled still remains,
> Deep-versed in books and shallow in himself,
> Crude or intoxicate, collecting toys
> And trifles for choice matters, worth a spunge;
> As children gathering pebbles on the shore.

> (Milton 1990: 495–96)

To what extent this rejection of Greek philosophy – indeed of reading itself – as the road to wisdom represents a public repudiation of the poet's own earlier humanism is still a matter of debate among Miltonists. In many ways, this English writer, product of one of the great humanist grammar schools, is the paradigmatic case of Protestant humanism, whose powerfully productive tensions and fusions permeate everything he wrote. Fluent in Latin and more than competent in Greek and Hebrew, he impressed the *literati* of the Florentine Academy with his idiomatic command of spoken and written Italian. His early writings, at least, are irradiated by Platonic idealism and a syncretic *allegoria* as bold as anything in Pico or Bruno. His role as intellectual conscience to Cromwell and the other leaders of the *coup d'état* of 1648–9 recalls that of Machiavelli with his Medici patrons, or More with the early Tudors. At the same time, Protestant conviction runs athwart the dialogical and controversial ethos of humanist debate. Christian truth may be elusive, embattled, difficult of access; but it is ultimately certain and indivisible, and Milton's texts cannot, in the last uncompromising analysis, entertain the heuristic openness, the commitment to the divergent and unruly truths of dialogue itself, that characterise the humanist mode.

In any case, in view of Milton's own assertion that there is a necessary distance between the poet and the person represented, it is probably unhelpful to read the speech too directly as an authorial manifesto, though it seems unlikely that he would have put into the mouth of the Son of God sentiments that he himself found entirely repugnant. What is clear is that the passage delivers a blow to the authority of the book no less damaging than Bacon's empirical methodology. True, it does so in the name of a book – the Bible – in whose authors are to be found all the qualities of wisdom, eloquence and aesthetic beauty claimed for Greek literature,

> As men divinely taught, and better teaching
> The solid rules of civil government
> In their majestic, unaffected style
> Than all the oratory of Greece and Rome.
> In them is plainest taught, and easiest learnt,
> What makes a nation happy, and keeps it so,
>
> (Milton 1990: 497)

and the treatment of scripture not as the fetishised 'word of God' but as a text of human (and multiple) authorship whose function is essentially educational and secular suggests that the lines of communication with humanist pedagogy have not been conclusively severed. For all its Guyon-like revulsion against the seductive languor of a classical eloquence 'thick laid / As varnish on a Harlot's cheek' (Milton 1990: 496), Milton's poem is not ready to be reclaimed by an irrational fundamentalist salvationism. Its rejection of the *docta ignorantia* ('educated ignorance') of the scholars and the bookish enthusiasms of the humanists (itself reminiscent of the humanist scepticism of Erasmus' *Praise of Folly* and Cornelius Agrippa's *De vanitate scientiarum* (*The Emptiness of Learning*)) comes not from some wild-eyed enthusiast but from a learned, bookish young Jew, fully capable of turning on the writings of the ancients their own weapons of scepticism and scorn:

> Think not but that I know these things; or, think
> I know them not, not therefore am I short
> Of knowing what I ought: he who receives
> Light from above, from the fountain of light,
> No other doctrine needs, thought granted true;
> But these are false, or little else but dreams,
> Conjectures, fancies, built on nothing firm.

(Milton 1990: 495)

But still, when all reservations have been made, and the humanist sources of Miltonic antihumanism fully acknowledged, this passage in the last book of his last poem remains a moment of significant rupture. The deliberate equivocation over whether the future Messiah has or has not read Plato and Aristotle ('Think not but that I know these things; or, think / I know them not') betokens not uncertainty but contemptuous indifference: the great preceptors of Athenian antiquity no longer have anything worthwhile to impart.

More tellingly still, their redundancy is delivered not by a superior scripture, a book (the Bible) that has the advantage of being true, but by a didactic that short-circuits the bibliocentric curriculum of the humanists entirely. *Deus illuminatio mea*: the triumphant divine illumination of Psalm 27 was the 'inner light' that guided the consciences of seventeenth-century Quakers and Anabaptists and emboldened them to challenge all book-derived authority, including the authority of scripture itself. For them, the voice of God spoke not through the learned translations and marginal glosses of an Authorised Version bearing the imprimatur of a hated Church and State, but directly to the vernacular heart of every simple, unlettered man or woman, in the glow of an inner illumination that signalled the immediate presence of divine truth. For all his praise of the 'majestic unaffected style' of the Hebrew patriarchs, the Miltonic 'light from above' is equally unconditional upon a textual mediation or a culture of literacy.

'Men divinely taught' need no books, and an 'unaffected style' of teaching can dispense with eloquence.

ENLIGHTENMENT

Milton's writings – the political prose of the republican 1640s and 1650s no less than the biblical poems published twenty years later – had great prestige in the century and a half following his death in 1674. Alongside the reverential piety of the politically and ecclesiastically orthodox, they circulated widely among radicals and freethinkers. One of the earliest biographies of the poet was by the republican and freethinker John Toland, author of the rationalistic *Christianity Not Mysterious* (1696). In France he enjoyed the admiration of Voltaire and of Mirabeau, who published a translation of his 1644 argument for an uncensored press, *Areopagitica*, in 1788, the year in which the States General convened to protest at royal and clerical despotism; while his 1651 *Defence of the English People*, justifying the trial and execution of Charles I, became in 1792 a call for the same treatment to be dispensed to the captive Louis XVI (Armitage et al. 1995: 254ff.). In pre-revolutionary America, Benjamin Franklin incorporated a passage from *Paradise Lost* into the personal liturgy he devised for domestic use, setting it to a hymn tune of his own composition, while his colleague Thomas Jefferson's commonplace book and private correspondence are full of Miltonic quotations and allusions (Armitage et al. 1995: 269). And Thomas Paine, who played a part in both the American and the French revolutions, ascribed his own deism and anticlericalism to his reading of Milton. In short, the blind poet who in 1667 had asked for 'Celestial Light' to

> Shine inward, and the mind through all her powers
> Irradiate, there plant eyes, all mist from thence
> Purge and disperse, that I may see and tell
> Of things invisible to mortal sight
>
> (Milton 1990: 201)

was himself enlisted as a powerful ally in the cause of what was already, by 1780, being called 'enlightenment'. Thus his work became – through ruptures and contradictions as much as continuities of transmission – a medium of transit between those humanist discourses of the sixteenth century, classical, aristocratic and backward-looking, in which he himself had been educated and which saturate his early writings, and the revolutionary and bourgeois humanism of the eighteenth century, with its manifesto of progressive rational enlightenment through the heroic endeavours of emancipated Man.

Like 'humanism', with which it will henceforth become closely associated, 'enlightenment' has a German pedigree. The trope itself was widely current in the eighteenth century: French *philosophes* (sceptical rationalists critical of the intellectual, clerical and sometimes political status quo) talked of a *siècle de lumières*, an age of illumination; Anglican clergymen with well-bred connections and comfortable rural livings deplored the narrow fanaticism of their dissenting neighbours, and congratulated themselves on their enlightened broad-mindedness; and Pope's epitaph for Isaac Newton ('Nature, and Nature's laws lay hid in night: / God said, Let Newton be! and all was light.') wittily rewrites the world-creating *fiat lux* of Genesis as a tribute to the illuminative powers of scientific reason (Pope 1956: 122). But it was the German philosopher Immanuel Kant, in an essay published in 1784 entitled *'Beantwortung der Frage: Was ist Aufklärung?'* ('Answer to the question: what is enlightenment?'), who gave the word its discursive authority, offering it as a normative description of the epoch:

> Enlightenment is the end of the self-imposed infancy of humankind ... *Sapere aude!* [Dare to know!] Thus the motto of enlightenment is, have the courage to follow your own understanding ... If it should be asked: do we live now in an enlightened age [*in einem aufgeklärten Zeitalter*]? the answer must be: no, but we surely live in an age of enlightenment [*in einem Zeitalter der Aufklärung*].
>
> (Kant 1867: 162)

The capitalisation of the noun and the use of the definite article, both normal in German, probably helped to promote the important slippage from the standard eighteenth-century attribute ('enlightenment') to the substantive abstraction ('the Enlightenment') that operates even today as a commonplace of intellectual history.

With this essay of Kant, writes his biographer, 'the philosophy of the Enlightenment has . . . reached its supreme goal' and 'finds its lucid, programmatic conclusion'.

> The evolution of mankind's spiritual history coincides with the progress, the ever keener comprehension, and the progressive deepening of the idea of freedom . . . [*Sapere aude!*] is at the same time the motto of all human history, for the process of self-liberation, the progress from natural bondage toward the spirit's autonomous consciousness of itself and of its task, constitutes the only thing that can be called genuine 'becoming' in the spiritual sense.
>
> (Cassirer 1981: 227–28)

Kant's project, which laid the foundations for the neo-humanism of von Humboldt and his colleagues, sought to construct a secure grounding for human knowledge that would not require an appeal to any authority beyond its own means of knowing. The history of philosophy from Bacon and Descartes to Kant and Hegel is characterised, it has been said, by a 'tendency . . . to replace ontology by epistemology' (Cassirer 1981: xv): that is, to replace questions about the world with questions about the mind, what exists with how that existence is known. While the Baconian investigator sets out to elicit the secret laws of nature, clearing his mind of the idols of prejudice in order to see more clearly what is actually there, Kant argues that there is nothing 'there' that has not been put there by the already-existing categories of thought. Reason does not observe nature; it constitutes it. With its strict separation of means and ends, its absolute distinction between the instrumental world of non-rational nature ('things') and the sovereign authority of rational humankind ('persons'), Kant's 'transcendental idealism' completes the theoretical demolition of religion, relocating its usurped authority within the human mind and will. 'Act only', states the 'categorical imperative' that governs all human conduct, according to that maxim by which you can at the same time will that it should become a universal law ... The practical imperative, therefore, is the following: Act so that you treat humanity, whether in your own person or in that of another, always as an end and never as a means only.

(Cassirer 1981: 245, 248)

'Enlightenment behaves towards things', remarks Adorno, 'as a dictator towards men. It knows them in so far as it can manipulate them.' Like the Florentine *umanisti* and their European pupils, whose writings rationalised the domestic and political culture of their princely patrons, the *philosophes* who promoted the humanistic values of enlightenment enjoyed a close if sometimes uncomfortable relationship with power. Rousseau's stormy involvement with the Commune of Geneva and Voltaire's symbiotic intimacy with the cultivated autocrats Catherine II of Russia and Frederick II of Prussia are the most obvious cases; but Helvétius, in a book (*De l'homme*, 1772) dedicated to Catherine II, wrote in praise of 'enlightened despotism'; and though not directly pensionary in the same way, Diderot, Hume and Kant (whom Heine called 'the Robespierre of the intellect', and who dedicated his *Universal Natural History* to Frederick II) saw themselves nonetheless as critics of benighted tyranny and superstition, and apostles of a new politico-intellectual order predicated on the universal axioms of human rationality and self-control.

The violent annals of European history provided few templates for such an ideal harmony of rational knowledge with absolute power, where a humanistic philosopher-prince, guided by a cabinet of sages, rules a contented populace with maxims derived from mathematics, music and natural theology. In their absence, Matteo Ricci's account, written at the turn of the sixteenth century, of the Confucian regime of the Ming emperors, amplified by later reports from the Jesuit mission and reinforced by the popularity of Chinese tea, textiles and porcelain, acquired wide currency. More even than the Greco-Roman model, disfigured as it was by violence and fanaticism, the example of China seemed to speak directly to the sensibility of the enlightened European.

Like his near-contemporary Socrates, Confucius taught his aristocratic pupils the sober virtues of moderation (the *chung hsui* or middle way), self-knowledge and the discipline of reason; but unlike the Greek, he insisted that those lessons must be put to practical use in government and public service. Thus while the former's imagined city, as recorded in the *Republic* of his pupil Plato, cannot exist outside the world of ideas, 'a pattern ... laid up in heaven for him who wishes to contemplate it' (*Republic* IX, 592B), the humanistic Confucianism of the Chinese empire had formed for two thousand years the practical curriculum of every school and the daily rule of life for millions. Small wonder if, to European intellectuals still haunted by the spectres of tyranny, revolution and the violence of the devout, China seemed

> the land of tolerance, of virtue without Christianity, of philosophical rulers with charming manners, of Deism, of reason triumphant: the very ideal to which Europe must strive to conform.
>
> (Cronin 1955: 278)

The Chinese protagonist of Oliver Goldsmith's *Citizen of the World* (1760) may be little more than a literary device, a knowingly innocent eye on the fads and follies of contemporary London; but in other hands the Chinese example could frame a powerful critique of European society. Surveying 'the condition of our affairs, slipping as we are ever into greater corruption', the Saxon philosopher-mathematician G.W. Leibniz proposed that, far from sending Jesuits to the East to peddle a superstitious and divisive Christianity, 'we need missionaries from the Chinese who will teach us the use and practice of natural religion' (Leibniz 1697: 10); while Voltaire opened his comprehensive *Essay on the Customs and Character of Nations* with a long and highly complimentary account of Chinese civilisation, the ideal and model of an enlightened despotism.

The central Confucian concept of *jen*, which combines the sense of 'humanity' with something closer to 'benevolence', has much in common with the western humanism which is the subject of this book. The latter, in this eighteenth-century context, still needs to be used parenthetically, since the word itself was not yet available. But the 'Man' around whom the discourses of enlight-enment are articulated, rational, sovereign and unconditional, betokens the emergence of a fully fledged humanism in all but name. Jonathan Swift's protest against the engulfing sentimen-tality of proto-humanist philanthropy ('all my love is towards individuals ... I hate and detest that animal called man; although I heartily love John, Peter, Thomas and so forth' [Swift, letter to Pope 24 Sept. 1725]) counts as nothing against his friend Pope's declaration in his *Essay on Man* that 'The proper study of mankind is man' (Pope 1956: 189).

Pope's polite deism ('presume not God to scan'), from which it is only a short step to the undisguised indifference of Edward Gibbon and the open atheism of David Hume, suggests the extent to which, since Milton, religious determinations, even when not explicitly repudiated, have lost all authority. The point can be made by contrasting the eighteenth-century usage with an earlier hypostatisation of 'Man': the condemnation or depreca-tion, generally with strong biblical associations, of human pride and folly. When Shakespeare's Isabella, in the accents of the pulpit, denounces 'man, proud man, Drest in a little brief authority, Most ignorant of what he's most assured' (*Measure for Measure* II, ii, 117–19), or his contemporary Ralegh invokes the figure of 'eloquent, just, and mighty Death' to rebuke 'all the far-stretched greatness, all the pride, cruelty, and ambition of man' (Ralegh 1614: V, v, 12), the impulse has nothing in common with 'humanism': a generalised 'man' is called up only to be exposed to a shrivelling judgement whose authority is still essentially theological. In contrast, though Kant may have retained all his life the Protestant pietism of his Prussian upbringing, the 'categorical imperative' that requires us unconditionally to treat other human beings as ends, not means, draws its warrant not from scripture but from the absolute sovereignty of secular reason. Diderot, without even the fig-leaf of a conventional piety, referred to Christianity with scorn as 'the Great Prejudice'; and Hume, who had been delighted, on a visit to France in 1765, to find 'almost universal Contempt of all Religion, among both Sexes, and among all Ranks of Men' (Gay 1970: 342), dismayed the sentimentally pious James

Boswell by declaring on his deathbed that his only regret was not to have completed the 'great work' of 'making his country-men wiser and particularly in delivering them from the Christian superstition' (ibid.: 341).

Earlier humanists had been suspected of unorthodoxy, even of infidelity, and most, including clerics like Erasmus and Bruno, were anticlerical, though rarely anti-religious. Even Hobbes and Locke observed the necessary protocols of piety, while scarcely bothering to conceal their lack of interest. It was the *Aufklärer* of the eighteenth century, armed (wrote Condorcet) with 'their battle-cry – *reason, tolerance, humanity*', who uncoupled the rhetoric of Man from the apparatus of creation myth and escha-tological anxiety that had encumbered it till then, and estab-lished the association between humanism and atheism which persists in the humanist associations and secular societies of the present day.

Nietzsche remarked that while 'the seventeenth century *suffers* from *humanity* as from a *host of contradictions*', the eighteenth 'tries to forget what is known of man's nature, in order to adapt him to its Utopia' (Hollingdale 1973: 97). 'Man' is articulated, now, not by but against religion; not within but apart from 'society'; not as a part, even a privileged part, of 'nature', but outside it. Rousseau's Man is born (not 'created') free, but immediately enchained by the shackles of a discredited social order. Nature, for Diderot as for Kant, derives its interest, indeed its meaningful existence, solely from the presence of rational Man:

> If mankind, or the thinking and contemplative beings which com-prise it, were banished from the surface of the earth, the moving and sublime spectacle of nature would be nothing more than a scene of desolation and silence. The universe would be mute; stillness and night would take possession of it ... It is the presence of man which renders other beings interesting, and what better consideration can we bring to bear in dealing with the history of such creatures? Why should we not introduce man into our work, as he has been placed in the universe? Why not make man the central focus?
>
> (Diderot 1992: 25)

'Man is the measure of all things': such, according to Plato, had been the doctrine of the philosopher Protagoras. Those eighteenth-century humanists who adopted it as their motto chose to overlook the moral relativism Protagoras deduced from it, and to ignore Socrates' clinical deconstruction of the rhetorical abstraction 'man', and the hopeless inconsistencies that follow from his substitution of 'you or I' for its hollow singularity. For them, as David Hume put it, 'There is no question of importance, whose decision is not compriz'd in the science of man' (Hume 1978: xvi), that transcendental figure who is defined in Diderot's *Encyclopedia* as 'the unique starting point, and the end to which everything must finally be related' (Diderot 1992: 293).

Of course, 'Tony Davies is the measure of all things' and 'John Drakakis is the end to which everything must finally be related' don't, for most people, have quite the same resonance. For one thing, they restore the forgotten gender, the historical lineaments of culture and class. In the figure of universal Man, the 'little a' of Hamlet's piece of work is finally erased; and the radical power of the figure, its truly revolutionary capacity, hangs on that erasure. Revolutions are fought in the name not of 'you or me', but of 'humanity'. Only later, when the job is done, do they disclose their hidden purposes. In getting rid of the deity, Sartre observed, the *philosophes* did not abandon the notion of a transcendental Being; they simply renamed it.

> In the philosophic atheism of the eighteenth century, the notion of God is suppressed, but not, for all that, the idea that essence is prior to existence; something of that idea we still find everywhere, in Diderot, in Voltaire and even in Kant. Man possesses a human nature; that 'human nature', which is the conception of human being, is found in every man; which means that each man is a particular example of an universal conception, the conception of Man.
>
> (Sartre 1948: 27)

This essentialism, which we might take as a precondition if not a definition of humanism itself, and which serves to differentiate it from earlier humanistic formulations of the figure, will last for two hundred years, and perhaps beyond. Even today, with its conceptual and political credibility in question, it persists in every common-sense appeal to human nature, to the 'central ... truly human point of view'. Like Crusoe cast adrift upon an indifferent nature by an oppressive society and an absentee Creator, enlightened Man, the only subject in a universe of objects, contemplates himself in the majestic solitude of his sovereign rationality, and broods upon the new world that awaits its creation.

5

THE END OF HUMANISM

> There is something in human history like retribution; and it is a rule of historical retribution that its instrument be forged not by the offended but by the offender himself.
>
> (Karl Marx)

> I'm a humanist; I'd rather kill a *man* than a snake.
>
> (Edward Abbey)

It must seem intolerably frustrating and perverse, to any reader quite reasonably looking for a clear, no-nonsense account of the matter, that a book on humanism has so far resisted the temptation to offer anything as straightforwardly helpful as a definition of the word, choosing instead to stress the plurality, complexity and fluidity of meanings it has been able to deploy or suggest. Indeed, if Humpty Dumpty is right – as he surely is – to insist that meaning is a form of mastery, not inherent in a word but torn from it in an unending struggle of definitions, then it may be that the meanings of 'humanism' have operated most powerfully precisely at those moments when they have been most contested, and thus most elusive or opaque to definition. In any case, I have chosen to explore the *how* and *why* of the various humanisms, their instrumentality and intentionality, leaving the *what* to the lexicographers. But the word insists on its due, and the time has come to acknowledge the responsibilities of authorship and the reasonable expectations of readers, and to attempt to seize the elusive beast of definition by the tail.

The root, appropriately, is a humble one: for both 'humble' and 'human' derive from the Latin *humus*, 'earth' or 'ground', from which all roots start; hence *homo*, earth-being, and *humanus*, earthy, human. Like all basic words, the human is defined oppositionally, by contrast with what it is not; in this case, with other earth-creatures (animals, plants) and with a higher order of beings, sky-dwellers or gods (*deus/divus, divinus*). By the time we get to late antiquity and the so-called 'Middle Ages', scholars and clerics have developed a distinction between *divinitas*, the fields of knowledge and activity deriving from scripture, and *humanitas*, those relating to the practical affairs of secular life. Even today the study of languages and literatures is still sometimes referred to as 'the humanities'; and since the latter drew much of their inspiration and their raw material from the writings of Roman and, increasingly, Greek antiquity, the (usually) Italian translators and teachers of those writings came, as we have seen, to call themselves *umanisti*, 'humanists'.

So far, the small constellation of words from which *humanism* will emerge looks reassuringly clear and technical: 'humanity' is that area of curricular knowledge that includes rhetoric, logic and the study of Greek and Roman authors – the arts of speaking and thinking, and the best examples of those arts; and a 'humanist' is someone who teaches those subjects or provides material for others who do so. But already at the outset complexity and muddle threaten. As early as the second century AD the Roman essayist Aulus Gellius was warning his readers against the dangers of confusion and vulgar sentimentality, and insisting that '*humanitas* does not mean what the common people think':

> Those who have spoken Latin and have used the language correctly do not give the word *humanitas* the meaning which it is commonly thought to have, namely, what the Greeks call *philanthropia*, signifying a kind of friendly spirit and good-feeling towards all men without

distinction; but they gave to *humanitas* about the force of the Greek *paideia*: that is, what we call, education and training in the liberal arts [*eruditionem institutionemque in bonos artes*]. Those who earnestly desire and seek after these are most highly humanized [*maxime humanissimi*]. For the pursuit of this kind of knowledge, and the training given by it, have been granted to man above all the animals, and for that reason it is termed *humanitas*, or 'humanity'.

(Gellius 1967: 457–58)

Sadly, Aulus' assurance that this 'is the sense that our earlier writers have used the word' won't stand up either, since there is plenty of evidence that classical authors, including his beloved and authoritative Cicero, were using *humanitas* freely in both its educational and its ethical senses at least two centuries before.

Aulus Gellius, writing in Athens and Rome during the *imperium* of Antoninus and Marcus Aurelius, stands near the head of those processes, cultural, political and linguistic, within which 'humanism' and 'the humanities' will later be generated; and already he anticipates many of their discursive dispositions – their élitism, their definitional purism, their tendency to identify the 'human' with the tastes and values of educated Europeans of a certain class. His *Attic Nights* were widely current in the fourteenth and fifteenth centuries, and helped shape the mental habits of the *umanisti* and their aristocratic pupils; to such an extent, indeed, that he becomes by adoption a 'Renaissance' writer, as much as an ancient one. Or perhaps even a modern, since his call to quarantine the 'original' meaning of *humanitas* against the infections of humanitarian sentiment and unlettered ignorance finds a curious echo much later, amid the ruins of another world-conquering empire, in the donnish etymologies of Martin Heidegger's 'Letter on Humanism':

It is precisely in these terms that *humanitas* is first defined and pursued. *Homo humanus* positions himself in opposition to *homo barbarus*. And *homo humanus* means in this instance the Roman, he who embodies Roman *virtus* and improves himself by 'colonising' what the Greeks called *paideia* ... *Paideia* in this sense is carried over into *humanitas* ... It is in Rome that we encounter the first humanism.

(Heidegger 1976: 320)

The 'Letter' was written in part to protest at the adoption of his own pre-war writings in support of the humanist existentialism of Jean-Paul Sartre, according to which, in Sartre's words, 'every man realises himself in realising a type of humanity' (Sartre 1948: 47). What Heidegger proposes for the word is an act of radical archaeological restoration, like the cleaning of an old painting, or the reconstruction of the ruined fabric of an ancient building:

> With regard to this more essential *humanitas* of *homo humanus* there arises the possibility of restoring to the word 'humanism' a historical sense that is older than its oldest meaning chronologically reckoned ... 'Humanism' now means, in case we decide to retain the word, that the essence of man is essential for the truth of Being, specifically in such a way that the word does not pertain simply to man as such.
>
> (Heidegger 1976: 345)

In other words, humanism remains usable as a philosophical concept, but only after it has been purged of the romantic and positivist anthropologies of 'man as such', and its connections with the semantic muddles of philanthropic 'humanity' irreparably severed.

These drastic realignments, which would wrench the word forcibly from its native habitat and isolate it in the purer air of a single essential and immutable meaning, would certainly simplify the problem of definition. Curiously, in view of its historical derivation, the manoeuvre is easier in German, where the relationship between *Humanismus* (humanism) and *Mensch/lichkeit* (humanity) is untroubled by family likeness (as it is in Heidegger's beloved Greek, which has no clear equivalent for *humanitas*), than it is in English and the romance languages, or Aulus' Latin, for that matter. But the contortions ('older than its oldest meaning') and hesitations ('in case we decide to retain the word') hint at the truth: that, alas, the quest for a single, original or even pre-original meaning is chimerical. The 'meaning' of humanism is a Snark ('For the Snark's a peculiar creature, that won't / Be caught in a commonplace way'), inseparable from the semantic tangle that makes its meanings so difficult to grasp. And the question of meaning belongs not to semantics but to politics, the definitional will-to-power, the question of 'which is to be master'; and that, even in the most authoritarian of linguistic tyrannies, is never unilateral or uncontested.

The case of Heidegger, around whom contemporary debates about humanism circle warily like dogs round a wounded bear, will serve as an example of just how much can be at stake in the seemingly simple matter of definition. Though his Hellenism and Teutonic nationalism identify him as a lineal heir of Humboldtian humanism, he strove in his critique of metaphysical and rhetorical error to position himself outside the assumptions of European thinking since Plato, and the anthropocentric illusion that lies at its heart, insisting that 'Man' is not the imperious subject but merely the object, the recipient, of 'Being', not the creator of language but its creature. At the same time, he contended that to reject the metaphysical humanism of post-Platonic thought, with its narrowly 'Roman' conception of what is human, in no way entails a repudiation of the common attachments and obligations of humanity itself. Philosophical antihumanism must not be confused with actual inhumanity.

> Because someone criticises 'humanism', people suspect a defence of the inhumane and a glorification of barbaric brutality. For what could be more 'logical' than to suppose that, for one who has said no to humanism, only the affirmation of inhumanity remains?
>
> (Heidegger 1976: 346)

Yet even here the ground is treacherous, since the Heidegger who wrote these words in 1947 had reason to know, better than most, that the conjunction of contemplative antihumanism with practical inhumanity could indeed on occasion have more substance than the vulgar confusion he castigates here. For the brilliant Rector of the University of Freiburg, who had so contemptuously repudiated his teacher Edmund Husserl and condoned the destruction of the careers, and perhaps the lives, of some of his own Jewish colleagues, did indeed deliver, in his 1936 inaugural address, 'a glorification of barbaric brutality'; not in so many words, to be sure, but in terms that unmistakably endorsed the *imperium* of the Master Race and lent it intellectual authority.

Heidegger was no unworldly innocent or opportunistic fellow traveller, but for several years an active and enthusiastic Nazi; and if the 'Letter on Humanism' and his other post-war writings can be read as an apologia, they are a frustratingly opaque and unapologetic one. Indeed, his turn against his former masters was prompted not by any revulsion at their unparalleled inhumanity but by the realisation that their rhetoric concealed an essentially Kantian (or Sartrean) *humanism*:

> The futility of Nazism becomes evident, however, once we recognise that it is precisely this humanistic tendency to treat humans as the ultimate goal, rather than as a means to achieving the authentic goal, that has created the sense of the aimlessness and nihilism of modern existence.
>
> (Guignan 1993: 34)

This Nietzschean insight recalls Adorno's identification of Nazism as the inner logic of humanist enlightenment, while also giving some support to his claim that Heidegger's thought was 'fascist in its most fundamental terms'. But Adorno, too, was not entirely innocent on this score, and his attack on his compatriot was perhaps prompted in part by guilty self-justification (Lacoue-Labarthe 1990: 117–18). In the matter of humanity, it seems, there are no clean hands. On the question of humanism, nothing could be more suspect than clarity.

WAITING FOR THE POST-MAN

'Man', that 'invention of recent date' who in Michel Foucault's conjecture 'may be nearing his end', is of course a philosophical entity, not a flesh-and-blood one: a creature of language and culture, 'invented' in the historically recent past and lately beginning to look a bit battered and disreputable. If the concept 'Man' is running out of time, it might seem that humanism must follow it into the historical dictionary and the museum of superannuated ideas. What word, if any, might take its place in a 'posthuman' or 'transhuman' lexicon of discourse then becomes an interesting question, one that has already generated some lively speculation. But before engaging with that, it is necessary to consider the possibility – some would already say probability – that humankind, which is indeed 'of recent date' in the chronology of terrestrial evolution, may actually have created or inherited the conditions of its – our – own quite literal and imminent extinction.

Several causes have been proposed, ranging from the apocalyptic day of wrath foretold in a number of ancient scriptures and the only slightly more credible invasion by a bug-eyed extraterrestrial life-form of irresistible power and malevolence, to the 'nuclear winter' that would follow a major thermonuclear war, replicating the effects of the monstrous volcanism or massive asteroid impact that are believed to have been responsible for earlier species' extinctions in the planet's history. But in recent years a prime suspect has been identified: 'Man' himself, who in his reckless 'enlargement of the bounds of empire' has consumed and degraded the resources of the Earth to such a degree that the finely balanced parameters of terrestrial life itself, the earth, air, fire and water of the ancients, have been thrown into chaotic and irreversible disorder. In this still disputed but menacingly plausible scenario, global temperature, driven by an accelerating spiral of greenhouse gas release, will within a few decades have melted the polar ice caps, raised the oceans and transformed tropical and temperate latitudes into arid wastelands scoured by storms, inundating large tracts of the Earth's land mass and rendering most of the remainder uninhabitable.

On the likely consequences for humanity, opinions differ. For some, *homo sapiens* is already condemned to follow other soon-to-be-extinct species such as the grey whale and black rhino, orang-utan and polar bear into the indifferent sediments of the fossil record. For others, the human species may cling to survival, but only at a terrible cost in mass famine, impoverishment and disease, and unending conflict over land, food and water: the coming to pass of that dystopian 'war of all against all' imagined by the seventeenth-century philosopher Thomas Hobbes, in which human life is 'solitary, poor, nasty, brutish and short'. This gloomy prediction has been given eloquent expression by the climate scientist James Lovelock, best known for his theory that the Earth is a holistic, self-regulating entity, whose every part, whether animate life or inanimate matter, is mutually inter-related with every other. This all-encompassing ecological system, to which Lovelock gives the mythological name Gaia, will always act to maintain or restore its overall equilibrium; and if that requires the creation of conditions in which a species cannot survive, so much the worse for the species.

Some will find a grimly satisfying logic in all this; for those same enlightenment sages, Hume, Diderot and Condorcet, who enthroned Man as the supreme principle and arbiter of the universe also fashioned the weapons that would topple him: weapons of scepticism, observation, hypothesis and experiment that over the following century would begin to unravel the true histories of stars, of terrestrial rocks and the creatures that cling to them, of the basic stuff of the universe, and of the consciousnesses that observe and ponder it all, creating narratives infinitely stranger, grander, more compelling than the cosmologies and ancestries supplied by myth or scripture. Taken all together, those narratives, of geology and paleontology, evolutionary biology, psychology and neurology, astrophysics and quantum mechanics, add up to a revolution in understanding, a revolution whose effect is to displace the human animal, Jared Diamond's 'third chimpanzee' (Diamond 1992), from the centre to the outer suburbs of existence; indeed, to displace the very notion of 'centre' that secures the conceptual scaffolding of the human. Just one species among millions, the majority far older, more numerous and more successfully adapted, on a pretty but insignificant planet orbiting an unimportant star in the outskirts of an undistinguished galaxy, Pico's Man is not the perfected master-piece of creation and heir to all its riches, but merely another of the uncountable myriads of transitional life-forms, part of the work-in-progress of the unending and unpredictable narrative of physical and organic evolution. For John Gray, man

> is only one of very many species, and not obviously worth preserving. Later or sooner it will become extinct. When it is gone the Earth will

recover. Long after the last traces of the human animal have dis-
appeared, many of the species it is bent on destroying will still be
around, along with others that have yet to spring up. The Earth will
forget mankind. The play of life will go on.

(Gray 2002: 151)

For many, the realisation that the sojourn of humanity is no
more than a minor episode in the continuing evolution of the
planet, that *homo sapiens* may turn out, on the long view of terrestrial life, to be no more than a temporary supply of food and
shelter for the true lords and inheritors of creation, the microbes
who were here three billion years before us and will doubtless
survive us by some billions more, brings a dismaying collapse of
morale. Victorian intellectuals, their belief in a benevolent deity
demolished by Darwin or Spencer, could at least revive their
spirits with a Comtean faith in human benevolence or a bracing
Nietzschean stoicism. And indeed, from that standpoint Gray's
or Lovelock's 'green dystopia' of planetary revenge and human
extinction may seem at first glance simply to rewrite earlier
premonitions of global disaster: the huge biblical and historical
canvasses of the Victorian painter-engineer John Martin depict-
ing the Flood of Genesis, the destruction of Babylon, the last
man on Earth, the end of the world; or the stark vision of a
human remnant clinging grimly to life in a world laid waste by
plague, war or alien invasion in Mary Shelley's *The Last Man*
(1826), Richard Jefferies' *After London* (1885) and H.G. Wells'
The War of the Worlds (1898). But these latest projections of
impending catastrophe ruthlessly strip away the consoling theology
of an angry but merciful creator, as well as its humanistic assurance that humanity will learn from the past and set about
rationally building a better world. For prophets of contemporary
catastrophe like Lovelock and Gray, the laws of physics, not those
of Moses or Mohammed, will determine the outcome; and while
survival on a small scale may be possible, it will be in wretchedly
hostile and impoverished circumstances, with no prospect of
anything better, ever: what Lovelock describes as 'global decline
into a chaotic world ruled by brutal warlords on a devastated
Earth'. From this desolate standpoint, the word 'human' starts to

sound like an accusation, and 'humanism' shrivels to the status of a noxious prejudice, like white supremacism; or worse, a querulous delusion, like creationism or scientology.

Written by scientists and supported by a compelling consensus of evidence and opinion, these bleakly terminal presentiments find their imaginative counterpart in the eschatological desparation of films like Mike Jackson's desolate *Threads* (1984) or George Miller's 1981 *Mad Max* sequel *The Road Warrior* ('In the future, cities will become deserts, roads will become battlefields and the hope of mankind will appear as a stranger'), and novels such as David Brin's *The Postman* (1985), Russell Hoban's haunting *Riddley Walker* (1980) and Cormac McCarthy's *The Road* (2006). Such stories speak to a deep unease, a sense that the human project, the very idea of humanity, is in real, maybe terminal, trouble, and that we have no one to blame but ourselves, no resources to call on but our own. These are the bad dreams of humanist triumphalism, nightmares with no prospect of waking, in which the technology we have learnt to rely on turns against us, our enemies are ruthless, invisible and everywhere, and the sources of life itself, air, water, sunlight, bread and meat, our fellow humans, have become the carriers of poison, disease and madness. Alarmingly, similar paranoid nightmares, with their lurid Manichaeism and millenarian bravado, now fuel the domestic policies and overseas excursions of the world's most powerful nations, intoxicated with the millenarian certainties of Christian Zionism and the impregnable rectitude of 'humanitarian intervention', and armed with the technology of global devastation and the jargon of pulp fiction, tabloid headlines and Playstation games: the War on Terror, the Clash of Civilisations, the Axis of Evil, Operation 'Shock and Awe'. Those adventures set out to save the civilised world ('*homo humanus*') from its enemies ('*homo barbarus*') under the venerable banners of liberty, decency and democracy: what Noam Chomsky (following Ulrich Beck) has called a 'new military humanism'. Chomsky is a linguist as well as a political activist, and his reaction to this latest expropriation of the slogans of enlightenment, like that of many liberals, is an essentially humanist rage against the pollution of public discourse, the prostitution of eloquence that precedes and justifies acts of official violence. Commenting on the air strikes on Kosovo by NATO forces in 1998, he writes that

> the events in Kosovo alone suffice to eliminate from consideration the primary and most exalted argument for the resort to force: that the NATO bombings, undertaken with humanitarian intent, open a new era in which the reigning superpower and its junior partner [the United States and Great Britain], suffused with previously-undetectable nobility, promise to lead the way to a new era of humanism and justice.
>
> (Chomsky 1999: 38)

Fuelled by outrage and invigorated by bitter irony, writing of this kind draws from a deep well of humanist protest. However close to despair, it clings to a residual belief in the possibility of persuasion, or at least of meaningful dialogue. For others, however, the only possible response to the lies and atrocities perpetrated in its name is a principled revulsion against humanity itself, in all its guises. Like Gulliver's decision to sleep in the stables with his horses in disgust at the vileness of his fellow Yahoos, John Gray's dissociative pronouns ('When it is [no*t* *we are*] gone the Earth will recover') enact a radical, if paradoxical, disavowal of humanity. 'I'm a humanist;' claimed the American environmentalist Edward Abbey, with sardonic intent, 'I'd rather kill a *man* than a snake', echoing the Californian poet Robinson Jeffers: 'I'd sooner, except the penalties, kill a man than a hawk' (Jeffers 1965, 'Hurt Hawks'; Abbey 1968: 7). For all three, the decisive conflict of modern times is no longer the confrontation between antagonistic human interests (workers and capitalists, whites and non-whites, fascists and democrats, women and men, old and young) but between the human species as a whole and the entire non-human world. Jeffers called this 'inhumanism': the 'shifting of emphasis and significance from man to notman'. For him, as for the political philosopher Gray and the scientist Lovelock, the truest perspective on the nature of things lies (in Nietzsche's phrase) 'beyond good and evil', beyond the squalid escapades of human greed and violence, in 'the recognition of transhuman magnificence'.

Outside the small circle of Jeffers enthusiasts, 'inhumanism' has never really caught on; sounds a bit too close to inhumanity, perhaps. But his other Nietzschean coinage, 'transhuman', has resurfaced in recent years, though in a context that Jeffers himself, a transcendental ruralist in the tradition of Thoreau and Emerson, might have winced at. In this later usage, too, imminent disaster or at least severe degradation, social, environmental, technological, is generally taken as given; but now human survival hangs on some heroic feat of technological mastery: the fusion of the human gene pool with a population of robotised cybermen armoured against the effects of global catastrophe, perhaps, or the departure of a little colony of pilgrim mothers (and the odd father) aboard an intergalactic *Mayflower*, in search of a new world on which to nurture the fragile future of humanity.

Here once again we enter territory in which the sober predictions of scientists and the plausible extrapolations of historians can be hard to distinguish from the unrestrained imaginings of fantasy fiction. Take Molly, for example, the glamorous 'street samurai' who accompanies the protagonist of William Gibson's 'cyberpunk' adventure *Neuromancer* on his violent and mysterious quest to unravel the secrets of cyberspace:

> The glasses were surgically inset, sealing her sockets. The silver lenses seemed to grow from smooth pale skin above her cheekbones. She held out her hands, palms up, the white fingers slightly spread, and with a barely audible click, ten double-edged, four-centimetre scalpel blades slid from their housings beneath the burgundy nails.
>
> She smiled. The blades slowly withdrew.
>
> (Gibson 1995a: 37)

Molly is only one of the cast of prosthetically enhanced transhumans who people Gibson's inventive and influential *Neuromancer* trilogy, including a 135-year-old who owes his longevity to 'a weekly fortune in serums and hormones' and 'a yearly pilgrimage to Tokyo, where genetic surgeons re-set the code of his DNA', a gangster whose 'eyes were vatgrown sea-green Nikon transplants', with his 'joeboys, nearly identical young men, their arms and shoulders bulging with grafted muscle', and the criminal entrepreneur Armitage, who has been rebuilt wholesale around the crushed and limbless torso of another man.

It would have been a mistake, even in 1984, to dismiss this kind of thing too readily as harmless fantasy. I am typing these words on a modestly priced, already elderly desktop machine with enough computing power to launch a moon landing, in a week in which the newspapers are reporting the first successful transplant of a human face, and a serious scientist (the 'head of futurology at BT' no less) assures us ('in deadly earnest') that by the middle of this century

> aeroplanes will be too afraid to crash, yoghurts will wish you good morning before being eaten and human consciousness will be stored on supercomputers, promising immortality for all.
>
> (*Observer* May 22 2005)

adding reassuringly (for younger readers) that 'by 2050 we would expect to be able to download your mind into a machine, so when you die it's not a major career problem'. Small wonder that since writing the *Neuromancer* sequence, Gibson has abandoned futuristic fiction as a hopeless enterprise, constantly upstaged or even anticipated by the morning's news.

The posthuman universe of Gibson's cyberpunk novels draws together a number of dystopian and futuristic motifs. The prosthetic amalgam called 'Armitage', for example, fictionally recycles the components of the original 'bionic man' Steve Austin, star of the 1973 TV series *The Six-Million-Dollar Man*, with its catchphrase 'We can rebuild him. We have the technology'; and that series in turn draws on an earlier sci-fi novel, Martin Caimin's *Cyborg*, itself a reworking of ideas that can be followed back to Wells. But more even than these, *Neuromancer*, a pungent collage of pulp-fiction themes and moods, caught, defined and perhaps helped create a moment, launching an idiom – cyberspace, the matrix – adopted by a generation of console cowboys, and splicing the argot and technology of arcade games, computer hackers and the (as yet uninvented) internet into the racy world of the private-eye thriller and the dystopian, paranoid milieu of Fritz Lang's *Metropolis* (1927) and George Orwell's *Nineteen Eighty-Four* (1949). Like those totemic fictions, it conceals beneath the hard-boiled swagger and transhuman decor a humanist pathos all the more poignant for its sense of abandonment and exile. Matthew Arnold's 'Ah love! Let us be true to one another' might be their motto; and Gibson's description of the writer's task, in a world in which memory, mother of the arts and patroness of the archive of humanity, has been mortgaged to the silicon brains on our desks and the great corporations that own them, rings with a plangent Arnoldian nostalgia:

> They go, they really do; we lose them totally as we move forward in this increasingly mediated existence. I think that's probably one of the tasks of the contemporary poet: to try to capture that sense of constant loss.
>
> (Gibson 1995b: 21)

Here the chronicler of posthuman cyberspace reveals himself as an unabashed Keatsian romantic, haunted by a lost, unrecoverable authenticity of unmediated experience. For others, however, it is that very *mediateness* of contemporary life, its inescapably prosthetic character, that offers the hope of survival, if not for humanity, then at least for 'posthumanity'. Only a degree of technical complexity, after all, separates a pair of spectacles, a hearing aid or an artificial leg from a new face, a whole-body transplant or a consciousness download. And if, as the classical humanists believed, my body is merely the vehicle, the disposable hardware, of my mind, consciousness or soul, of all the things that make me authentically human, then what shall we call the machine that houses those things when the rest of me has gone to the transplant warehouse?

This is the perspective of Donna Haraway's 'Cyborg Manifesto', which asks us to think of ourselves and the world around us not in terms of 'bodies', fixed entities with stable boundaries, but of assemblies of parts, fluid, diverse and interchangeable:

> Taking responsibility for the social relations of science and technology means refusing an anti-science metaphysics, a demonology of technology, and so means embracing the skilful task of reconstructing the boundaries of daily life, in partial connection with others, in communication with all of our parts. It is not just that science and technology are possible means of great human satisfaction, as well as a matrix of complex determinations. Cyborg imagery can suggest the way out of the maze of dualisms in which we have explained our bodies and our tools to ourselves.
>
> (Haraway 2000: 84)

To do this will require an effort to think and feel beyond the antinomies (I/you, mind/body, nature/culture) that subtend so many of our ideas, including ideas of the human. If someone else's kidney keeps me alive, or her cornea cures my blindness, that does not make me in any degree that other person, any more than a pig's liver makes me a pig or a heart pacemaker a machine. But it might make me think in unfamiliar ways about what 'me' means, and how much else of 'me' (my genes? my molecules? my favourite music? my ideas about humanism?) is on loan from elsewhere. For Haraway, we are all 'cyborgs', constantly in and out of each other's minds and bodies, borrowing each other's parts and tools, existing only in the interplay of self and non-self: denizens 'not of a common language, but of a powerful infidel heteroglossia' (Haraway 2000: 84).

For Katherine Hayles, too, the fluidity of meanings and identities in a post/transhuman world should be welcomed as a way of escaping the monoglot tyranny of definition:

> The best possible time to contest for what the posthuman means is now, before the trains of thought it embodies have been laid down so firmly that it would take dynamite to change them. Although some current versions of the posthuman point toward the antihuman and the apocalyptic, we can craft others that will be conducive to the long-range survival of humans and of the other life-forms, biological and artificial, with whom we share the planet and ourselves.
>
> (Hayles 1999: 291)

It is not irrelevant to note that both the passages just quoted, with their strikingly upbeat tone, were written by women. Given the predominantly masculine character of the humanist enterprise, and of the societies that have sustained it and shaped its terms, women have always had an ambiguous stake in the universalising assertions of male humanists, and a keener consciousness of the contradictions and equivocations (sometimes, the plain lies) that underlie them. Perhaps for that reason, feminist scholars like Hayles and Haraway have led the debate for a dissident ('infidel') and pluralised ('heteroglot') posthumanity, just as novelists like Doris Lessing (*Canopus in Argos*, 1979–83), Ursula Le Guin (*The Left Hand of Darkness*, 1969) and Joanna Russ (*The Female Man*, 1975) have developed the genres of fantasy and sci-fi in ways that allow them to explore the problematics of (trans)human survival without falling into the boy's-toys technolatry and erotic reveries, or apocalyptic gloom of their male contemporaries.

It should be clear by now that all these prospectives for posthumanity, like the antihumanisms discussed earlier, serve unmistakably humanist, indeed enlightenment, ends of understanding and emancipation. Humanism can be historicised, critiqued, deconstructed, pluralised, held to account, but it is not yet ready, it seems, to be left behind: a chastened humanism, to be sure, shorn of its swagger and self-righteousness, its ears still ringing with Nietzschean mockery, its conscience troubled by ancestral guilt, but a kind of humanism nonetheless.

TOWARDS A CONCLUSION . . .

So it seems after all that there will not be any tidy definitions, nor indeed could there be. The several humanisms – the civic humanism of Confucian sages and quattrocento Italian city-states, the Qur'anic humanism of Ibn Sina and Ibn Rushd, the Protestant humanism of sixteenth-century northern Europe, the rationalistic humanism that served the revolutions of enlightened modernity, and the romantic and positivistic humanisms through which the European bourgeoisies established their hegemony over it, the revolutionary humanism that shook the world and the liberal humanism that sought to tame it, the humanism of the Nazis and the humanism of their victims and opponents, the antihumanist humanism of Heidegger and the humanist anti-humanism of Foucault and Althusser, the secularist humanism of Huxley and Dawkins or the posthumanism of Gibson and Haraway – are not reducible to one, not even to a single, tidy line or pattern. Each has its distinctive historical curve, its particular discursive poetics, its own problematic scansion of the human. Each seeks, as all discourses must, to impose its own answer to the question of 'which is to be master'.

Meanwhile, the question of humanism remains, for the present, an inescapable horizon within which all attempts to think about the ways in which human beings have lived, do live, might live together in and on the world are contained. Not that the actual humanisms described here necessarily provide a model, or even a useful history, least of all for those very numerous people, and peoples, for whom they have been alien and oppressive. Some, at least, offer a grim warning. Certainly it should no longer be possible (though of course it is) to formulate phrases like 'the ascent of man' or 'the triumph of human reason' without an instant consciousness of the presumption and brutality they drag behind them.

All humanisms, until now, have been imperial. They speak of the human in the accents and the interests of a class, a sex, a race, a genome. Their embrace suffocates those whom it does not ignore. The first humanists scripted the tyranny of the Borgias, Medicis and Tudors. Later humanists dreamed of freedom and celebrated Frederick II, Bonaparte, Bismarck, Stalin. The liberators of colonial America, like the Greek and Roman thinkers they emulated, owned slaves. At various times, not excluding the present, the circuit of the human has excluded women, those who do not speak Greek or Latin or English, those whose complexions are not pink, Jews, Arabs, children. It is almost impossible to think of a crime that has not been committed in the name of humanity.

At the same time, though it is clear that the master narrative of transcendental Man has outlasted its usefulness, it would be unwise simply to abandon the ground occupied by the historical humanisms. For one thing, some variety of humanism remains, on many occasions, the only available alternative to bigotry and persecution. The freedom to speak and write, to organise and campaign in defence of individual or common interests, to protest and disobey: all these, and the prospect of a world in which they will be secured, can only be articulated in humanist terms. It is true that the Baconian 'Knowledge of Causes, and Secrett Motions of Things', harnessed to an overweening rationality and an unbridled technological will to power, has enlarged the bounds of human empire to the point of endangering the survival of life on the violated planet on which we live. But how, if not by mobilising collective resources of human understanding and responsibility, of 'enlightened self-interest' even, can that danger be acknowledged, confronted, perhaps even turned aside?

The Jewish philosopher Emmanuel Levinas has written of the possibility of an *'humanisme de l'autre homme'*, a concept and practice of the human that proceeds not – like Descartes' self-contemplative 'I' or Kant's transcendental subjectivity – from a primary centred subjectivity reaching out to know and seize the world, but from the ethical recognition of an irreducible 'Other', the not-I that defines me for myself. Levinas retraces here the gesture of those structuralist and posthumanist thinkers like Saussure, Lévi-Strauss, Foucault and the psychoanalyst Jacques Lacan, for whom the speaking, conscious 'I' is always provisional and secondary to the orders of language and social meaning within which it constructs itself. But his writing, though refreshingly free of the complacent philanthropic piety of much contemporary humanism, is grounded in an ethical register denied to those for whom the human is simply an effect of structure or discourse. Humanity is neither a given essence nor an achievable end, but a continuous and precarious process of becoming human, a process that entails the inescapable recognition that our humanity is on loan from others, to precisely the extent that we acknowledge it in them. For those 'westerners' whose humanness is mortgaged to the suffering and labour of an innumerable 'Other', the recognition cannot be comfortable or merely reflective. The humanity of Prospero is defined – conferred, conditioned – by Caliban; and the implications for both are political no less than philosophical.

For some even this will not be enough. More than one reader of Heidegger has noted that his rigorous antihumanism takes him only as far as the conceptual frontier that divides the human from the animal, at which point 'the revolution in thought comes to a halt and the deep currents of humanism reassert themselves' (Steeves 1999: 25); and Levinas' Other, though categorically unknowable, confronts the ethical consciousness as a 'face', an absent presence we can only imagine as human. Like it or not, we are all Darwin's children, and should hardly need the work of animal rights theorists like Peter Singer to remind us that the distinction between 'man' and 'beast' is every bit as flimsy, as historically contingent, as open to question as the other dualistic boundary-markers (man/god, man/machine, man/alien) that have served to define and confine the 'human'.

There is a poem by Ted Hughes, 'Wodwo', that hauntingly re-creates the process of becoming human. A creature – a voice, a consciousness, a sense of touch and smell – is exploring its environment, feeling for texture and response, mapping the fluid boundaries of identity.

> I seem to have been given the freedom
> of this place what am I then? And picking
> bits of bark off this rotten stump gives me
> no pleasure and it's no use so why do I do it
> me and doing that have coincided very queerly
> But what shall I be called am I the first
> have I an owner what shape am I what
> shape am I am I huge if I go
> to the end on this way past these trees and past these trees
> till I get tired that's touching one wall of me

The poem is about identity as movement, not destination; seeking, not finding. There is no climactic discovery of self, and the ending lacks the closure of, say, Browning's 'Caliban upon Setebos', a poem to which it bears a superficial resemblance ('Will sprawl, now that the heat of day is best, Flat on his belly in the pit's much mire'):

> for the moment if I sit still how everything
> stops to watch me I suppose I am the exact centre
> but there's all this what is it roots
> roots roots roots and here's the water
> again very queer but I'll go on looking

(Hughes 1964: 183)

It might be a baby, an early hominid, the mutilated and mutant survivor of some global devastation, groping towards language and consciousness. Hughes himself has described it as

> some sort of satyr or half-man or half animal, half all kinds of elemental little things, just a little larval being without shape or qualities who suddenly finds himself alive in this world at any time.

(Sagar 1975: 98)

The Wodwo, a wild forest-dwelling creature borrowed from the Middle English poem *Sir Gawain and the Green Knight*, is at once ourselves (the infant or ancestor we carry within us) and everything that is not ourselves (the prehuman, the savage, the brute). But the figure resists both the romantic infantilism of Wordsworth's 'Immortality Ode' and the primitivism of Lawrence's animal poems (both important forebears for Hughes), allowing its own proto-humanity to emerge as if recognised for the first time, through words that are at once ordinary and utterly strange; an Ovidian metamorphosis in reverse, speechless matter feeling towards a voice and a shape.

Hughes, who included a poem about Sartre in the collection that takes its title from 'Wodwo', might almost have been thinking of the French philosopher's critique of the Enlightenment figure of universal Man, that abstraction that insists that

> each man is a particular example of an universal conception, the conception of Man. In Kant, this universality goes so far that the wild man of the woods, man in the state of nature and the bourgeois are all contained in the same definition and have the same fundamental

qualities ... the essence of man precedes that historic existence which we confront in experience.

(Sartre 1948: 27)

But for an even more telling commentary on the poem, we can turn to an essay by Jean-François Lyotard, best known as the pioneering cartographer of the 'postmodern condition', in which he ponders the boundary lines that have been drawn between the human and its cultural antonyms – non-human, pre-human, inhuman, sub-human. Is it a question, he asks, reformulating Rousseau's postulate of a primal freedom, of a creature born human, only to learn inhumanity from its fellow humans? Or is it humanity that we learn, in that painful journey into language and social existence?

What shall we call human in humans, the initial misery of their childhood, or their capacity to acquire a 'second' nature which, thanks to language, makes them fit to share in communal life, adult consciousness and reason?

(Lyotard 1991: 3)

For Lyotard, there can be no final resolution of the dilemma: it is precisely the oscillation between the two definitions, between 'biological' and 'cultural' humanities, that constitutes the question of the human. But his account of the newborn infant has a pathos that irresistibly recalls Hughes' 'elemental little thing', and seems both to endorse the humanity of the not-yet-human and to arraign the inhumanity of the human world in which it finds itself:

Shorn of speech, incapable of standing upright, hesitating over its objects of interest, not able to calculate its advantages, not sensitive to common reason, the child is eminently the human because its distress heralds and promises things possible. Its initial delay in humanity, which makes it the hostage of the adult community, is also what manifests to this community the lack of humanity it is suffering from, and which calls on it to become more human.

(Lyotard 1991: 3–4)

'Wodwo', likewise, offers no Kantian solidarity with the essentially human, no consoling recognition of a shared condition. The poem inhabits a world beyond (before, after) humanism, in which the human can no longer be taken for granted, but must be rediscovered anew in each encounter with a ceaselessly changing reality. For the heirs and curators of European humanism, on whom, as Marx said, 'the tradition of the dead generations weighs like a nightmare' (Marx 1973b: 146), the task of defining humanity has passed elsewhere. Others will tell us if we are human, and what it means. Whether that will lead in turn to new humanisms, and whether they will be less imperious and exclusive than the old, it may be too early, or perhaps too late, to say.

Glossary

Adab   'Right conduct' in Arabic, and still an important concept in contemporary **Islam**, where it is widely taught as the indispensable
foundation for a young person's ethical, intellectual and civic
development, *adab* was central to the Arab 'renaissance' of the
ninth and tenth centuries, where its role closely resembled that of
both the ancient Greek *paideia* and the Latin *humanitas* (see p. 127),
and can thus be seen as analogous to the broader ethical uses of
humanism.

Altruism   Coined by English followers of Auguste Comte to express his
notion of acting '*pour autrui*' (in the interests of the other), altruism
soon developed its wider sense of unselfishness, the antonym of
egoism.

Antihumanism   Principled opposition to the idea that human values and
interests should be central to our understanding of, and life in, the
world. Antihumanism can have a number of groundings: religious
(or quasi-religious): we owe our existence to a higher being or
force, who/which demands our respect and obedience; philosophical: humanism is a delusion of freedom and significance, easily
exposed as such by a proper understanding of language
(Nietzsche), psychology (Freud) or history (Althusser); ethical:
humanism is a form of collective narcissism, blind to its own folly,
absurdity and cruelty (Gray); and scientific: on evolutionary and
cosmological scales, human existence is too recent and almost
certainly too short-lived to be either central or particularly significant in the history of the planet or the universe (Lovelock, Gray).
In one or other of these senses, antihumanism informs artistic
modernism (pp. 46–8), much twentieth-century philosophy (pp.
54–9) and contemporary ecological thinking (pp. 131–6). Some of
them, at least, retain humanist *ends* (though not means) of rational
understanding and intellectual freedom.

Atheism   The conviction that there is no deity or other supernatural
entity in charge of the universe or of human affairs (Greek *a-theos*:
'no god'). In earlier centuries the word was used more loosely to

describe religious heresy or scepticism, but from the nineteenth century onwards, driven by increasingly powerful scientific evidence that the biblical account of the creation of the world could not possibly be true, it assumed the stricter sense of principled unbelief, in close companionship with the first formally humanist organisations (see **secularism**). The fact that certain well-known contemporary atheists display all the missionary fervour, certitude and intolerance of old-time religion is taken by some as evidence that those qualities are not a monopoly of the devout.

Cartesian Characteristic of, or deriving from, the writings of the French philosopher and mathematician René Descartes (Cartesius). The term is used particularly of the mind–body dualism that flows from his declaration that 'I think, therefore I am' (sometimes called the *cogito* from its Latin form: *'cogito, ergo sum'*).

Copernican The Polish astronomer Nicolaus Copernicus (1473–1543), though not the first to challenge the common view that the Earth was at the centre of the universe, provided mathematical and observational proofs that it orbited the sun in common with the other planets (*De revolutionibus orbium coelestium* 1543). This 'decentring' of the Earth, and therefore of humankind, has given its name metaphorically to later 'Copernican' endeavours such as Lyell's *Principles of Geology* (1830), Darwin's *Origin of Species* (1859), Marx's *Capital* (1867) and Freud's *Interpretation of Dreams* (1900).

Cyberspace First used in a story by William Gibson, cyberspace has been widely adopted as the name of the spacially limitless 'virtual' territory mapped out by computers and the networks that connect them, including the internet. Gibson's own definition is both conceptually wider (he includes among the denizens of cyberspace 'children being taught mathematical concepts') and more sceptical (he calls it 'evocative and essentially meaningless').

Cyborg A human being prosthetically enhanced or hybridised with electronic or mechanical components which interact with its own biological systems. For some **posthumanists** the cyborg is a metaphor for the increasing and necessary interdependency of humans and machines, especially computers (see also **transhumanism**).

Determinism The view that all events have a predetermining cause, and that their occurrence is therefore inevitable and, if the cause is fully understood, predictable. Though many religious traditions, with their ideas of destiny and divine foreknowledge, are deterministic, modern determinisms model themselves on the sciences. Some versions of Marxism, for instance (though not Marx's own), offer a historical determinism, in which the 'laws' of historical development are as inexorable as the laws of classical physics or chemistry.

Dystopia   Coined by John Stuart Mill to describe 'something . !. too bad to be practicable', dystopia is the ugly sister of utopia: an imaginary place or world characterised by misery, injustice, oppression and hopelessness. Most utopias would turn out to be dystopias if we actually had to live in them.

Empiricism   The view that all knowledge derives from concrete experience, and specifically from the five senses. More broadly, and against both idealism (the theory that we only know ideas of things, not things themselves) and rationalism (which holds that knowledge comes not from experience but through rational argument and proof), empiricism describes a kind of 'common sense', non-theoretical view of the world, a view which is sometimes thought to be typically Anglo-Saxon.

Enlightenment   In general terms, the rejection of religious and pseudo-scientific superstition in favour of rational understanding, investigation and proof. Although originally a religious concept (the divinely implanted 'light within' of European Protestants), it became in the eighteenth century the watchword of religious sceptics and non-believers and gave its name to the (rough) century from John Locke's *Essay Concerning Human Understanding* (1690) to the battle of Trafalgar (1805), and which included the lifetimes of Voltaire, Rousseau and Hume, the American and French revolutions, and the publication of Paine's *Rights of Man*.

Essentialism   The view that any idea, experience or mode of existence can be referred back to, and explained by, its 'essence': a fundamental, unchanging and irreducible quality that makes it what it is. This is what we are doing when, in ordinary language, we say that two apparently different things are 'essentially the same'. Most humanisms are essentialist, since they take for granted the existence and integrity of the 'human'.

Existentialism   A radical **individualism** which holds that human beings give meaning (or non-meaning) to their lives by the choices they make and the actions that flow from them. Drawing on the work of

Nietzsche and the Danish theologian Søren Kierkegaard, Jean-Paul Sartre and Simone de Beauvoir developed a strongly political existentialism which, though initially humanistic (*Existentialism Is a Humanism*, 1946), soon embraced Marxism and anti-colonialism and turned against humanism ('nothing but an ideology of lies', Sartre 1961).

Hellenism   Admiration, often amounting to veneration, for the literature, culture and way of life of the ancient Greeks, particularly the Athenians of the sixth and fifth centuries BCE, regarded as an ideal model to which all societies and individuals should aspire.

Heteroglossia   The idea, associated with the Russian linguist and cultural theorist Mikhail Bakhtin, that every utterance, however simple or authoritative, contains within itself a number of different and often competing 'accents', representing different viewpoints, interests and experiences of the world.

Historicism   A form of historical **determinism** and/or **essentialism** which holds that history has a logic, direction and purpose independent of the wishes and actions of individuals.

Humanism   An undefinable term, possibly obsolete.

Humanist   A teacher and writer of books. A superman. A deluded wretch, deserving pity and contempt. None of the above. All of the above.

Individualism   The view that individual human beings are in their essential beliefs, choices and actions independent and self-responsible. Individualism is an important element of **Enlightenment** rationalism, and underpins both **liberal humanism** and the 'greed is good' ethos of contemporary capitalism.

Islam   The word means 'submission' (to the will of Allah, as revealed in the sixth century CE to his prophet Muhammad), and Muslims ('those who have submitted') see Islam not as a separate religion but as the final realisation of the monotheistic and prophetic tradition initiated by Abraham, Moses and Jesus, all three revered in the Qur'an as prophets. This ecumenical openness towards Judaism and Christianity extended also to the writings of Plato and Aristotle, translated into Arabic in the later sixth century, which in turn inspired a five-hundred-year humanistic 'renaissance' in Baghdad, Isfahan, Cordoba and other intellectual centres of the Islamic world. Weakened by Mongol invasions from the north-east and

Shi'ite zealotry within, this movement was fatally damaged by the Crusades, which presented western Christians not as a kindred 'people of the Book' but as brutal and implacable imperialists.

Jen 'Humanity' in both its senses ('human-ness' and compassionate fellow feeling): a central concept in the teachings of Confucius (Kung fu Tze), the foundation of both individual goodness and civic responsibility.

Liberal humanism The 'liberal' in liberal humanism defines the human in Enlightenment terms: every human being is an autonomous individual endowed with natural rights, talents and responsibilities and the rational means to realise them to the fullest extent. Most modern humanisms (and humanists) are liberal in this sense, and some version of liberal humanism underpins almost all modern societies and political parties, left or right, except those organised around religious doctrines.

Modernism An artistic and intellectual movement in the first half of the twentieth century, anti-romantic, anti-humanist, generally anti-democratic, hostile to interpretation, and committed to radical purity and simplicity of form and the uncompromising objectivity of the created work. Politically ambivalent but often authoritarian in spirit, modernism gave us the paintings of Picasso, Léger and Braque, the poems of T.S. Eliot and Ezra Pound, the music of Bartók and Stravinsky and the architecture of Le Corbusier.

Neoplatonism Plato's ideas about the immortality of the soul, and its cyclical return at death to the transcendent source of knowledge and being, were developed by later Platonists into a mystical and allegorical philosophy that was taken up by early Christian theologians, as well as by Muslim and Jewish intellectuals like Al-Farabi and Maimonides. The rich **syncretic** mix of monotheistic mysticism and Platonic idealism is an important influence on Florentine humanists like Marsilio Ficino and Pico della Mirandola.

Philology The historical study of languages and (in broader usage) their vernacular literatures, seen by nineteenth-century philologists as a royal road into the collective consciousness and 'soul' of a people. Though academic philology has now largely given way to analytic linguistics, a book like Martin Bernal's *Black Athena* (1987–2006), on the African and Asiatic roots of Greek language and culture, suggests that it can still frighten the chickens.

Platonism The publication in the fifteenth century of the Greek text of Plato's dialogues made it possible to disentangle his writings from the exotic elaborations of **neoplatonism**. Renaissance and later Platonists took up the Athenian's *psychology*, which proposes that our knowledge of the world is a partial reminiscence of the absolute knowledge our souls possessed before they entered the world of birth, time and death, and the related *epistemology*, according to which every concrete object of thought is merely the crude representation of an imperishable idea, imperfectly remembered. For the Platonist, the purpose of philosophy (of life, in fact) is to recover as fully as possible the ideas (of justice, beauty, love, virtue) that animate the objects of everyday knowledge.

Positivism The view, pioneered by Auguste Comte (and pilloried by Charles Dickens), that the only valid knowledge is the knowledge of positive facts, established by the application of scientific reasoning to experimental and **empirical** data. Comte, who invented the word 'sociology', was primarily interested in the understanding of human society. Others have extended positivist principles to the natural sciences, psychology, and even literature and the visual arts.

Posthumanism As with **postmodernism**, the 'post' signifies both continuity and rupture: continuity in its ongoing preoccupation with humanist themes of identity, liberty and **secular** morality; rupture in its rejection of the privileged position accorded to humankind among other concepts and life forms. Many posthumanists are open to the **transhuman** enlargement of human potential through the use of technology, but most prefer to think of the human future in ethical and cultural terms, as a responsible and neighbourly cohabitation with our fellow species.

Postmodernism Both the successor to, and a sharp critique and rejection of, **modernism**: the successor to modernism's determination to 'make it new' (Ezra Pound), to find forms and idioms that embody contemporary experience; but a critique of its supposedly monolithic character, its elitism and cult of difficulty, its contempt for popular culture and everyday life.

Rationalism The view that we derive knowledge of the world neither from the **empirical** evidence of our senses nor from pre-existing ideas or mental structures, but through rational deduction and analysis from verifiable data. For the rationalist, large, complex bodies of knowledge can be derived purely by deduction from one or two simple proofs, on the analogy of Euclid's geometrical theorems.

Reformation A movement in fourteenth- and fifteenth-century Europe, especially Bohemia, Moravia, Germany and the Low Countries, to challenge the overarching power of the Church of Rome and to restore the doctrine, liturgy and practice of Christianity to the apostolic simplicity recorded in the Gospels, Acts and Epistles. Many of the leading reformers were humanists, and some (Martin Luther in Germany, John Knox in Scotland, Thomas Cranmer in England) founded independent churches, sometimes called 'Protestant' after Luther's *protestatio* (protestation) against Roman Catholic authority, which survive to this day.

Renaissance The word, which means 'rebirth', was coined in the nineteenth century to describe the revival of Greek and Latin scholarship in Italian and other European city states in the fourteenth and fifteenth centuries, and its impact on the style and subject-matter of painting, sculpture, architecture and the decorative arts. The classical revival coincided with, and was greatly assisted by, the development of printing with movable type, and was promoted by a network of professional educators called *humanists* (*umanisti*).

Secularism The belief that the institutions of public and private life should be entirely free from the influence or interference of religion. Despite spending six months in jail for blasphemy, George Holyoake, the Victorian freethinker who coined the word, stopped short of attacking religious belief, which he regarded as a matter for individual judgement; but many later secularists (in effect, **atheists**) would argue that religious belief is irrational and divisive, and has no place in modern society.

Sharia Literally 'path', like the Chinese *tao*, *sharia* is the body of Islamic law and the principles underlying it, derived from the Qur'an, and the *hadith* and *sunna*, the recorded sayings and actions of Muhammad.

Structuralism Any method of analysis (in linguistics, anthropology, psychology for example) that looks not at the immediate data (words, social customs, behavioural symptoms) but at the underlying elements and interrelationships, the structural grammar, of which they are the expression.

Syncretism The bringing together into a single discourse of elements from different (especially religious) traditions and belief systems.

Renaissance Platonists like Pico della Mirandola drew on the similarities between Greek, Roman, Christian, Zoroastrian and Muslim theologies, arguing that all were versions of a single **essential** truth.

Theodicy   The view that God is all-knowing and all-powerful, and that all his (rarely: her) actions are without exception justified and justifiable, even when they cause suffering and appear to perpetuate the existence of evil.

Transhumanism   'Trans' as in transform or transcend: transhumanism takes up Nietzsche's call for humankind to rise above its historic limitations and reinvent itself as a super-species. Nietzsche was concerned with intellectual transcendence. Contemporary transhumanists look to science (prosthetics, cryonics, genetics and nanotechnology) to create a biotechnological *Übermensch* who will, to quote one of them, 'combine the qualities, say, of Einstein, Shakespeare, Mozart, Darwin, J.M.W. Turner, a nuthatch and a pocket calculator'. Aspiring nuthatches can find out more at www.aleph.se/Trans.

Utilitarianism   The view, associated with the philosopher Jeremy Bentham (though the word was coined by his godson John Stuart Mill), that the primary motivation for human beings is the pursuit of pleasure (the satisfaction of basic needs and desires) and the avoidance of pain (the deprivation of those things). It follows that the ethical touchstone of every private action or public policy, the test of its ethical and practical 'utility', is that it should promote 'the greatest happiness of the greatest number'. The 'felicific calculus' (Mill's phrase) has subsequently been extended to other living creatures, and Peter Singer has based an argument for animal rights on utilitarian principles (Singer 1990).

REFERENCES AND RELATED READING

Abbey, Edward (1968) *Desert Solitaire*, New York: Ballantine

Adorno, Theodor W. (1973) *The Dialectic of Enlightenment*, trans. John Cummings, London

Alighieri, Dante (1981) *Literature in the Vernacular*, translated by Sally Purcess, Manchester

Althusser, Louis (1969) *For Marx*, trans. Ben Brewster, Harmondsworth: Penguin

Arendt, Hannah (1958) *The Human Condition*, Chicago: University of Chicago Press

Armitage, David, Himy, Armand and Skinner, Quentin (1995) *Milton and Republicanism*, Cambridge: CUP

Arnold, Matthew (1869) *Culture and Anarchy*, London

——(1888) *Essays in Criticism: Second Series*, London

Ascoli, A.R. and Kahn, V. (1993) *Machiavelli and the Discourse of Literature*, Ithaca, NY

Auerbach, Erich (1968) *Mimesis*, trans. Willard R. Trask, Princeton, NJ: Princeton University Press

Bacon, Francis (1905) *Philosophical Works*, ed. J.M. Robertson, London

——(1974) *The Advancement of Learning and New Atlantis*, ed. Arthur Johnston, Oxford: OUP

Barrett, Michèle (1991) *The Politics of Truth: From Marx to Foucault*, Oxford: Blackwell

Bernal, Martin (1987) *Black Athena*, London

Biddiss, M.D. (1970) *Father of Racist Ideology: The Social and Political Thought of Count Gobineau*, London

Blackham, H.J. (1976) *Humanism*, Hassocks: Sussex University Press

Bond, Edward (1978) 'The Rational Theatre', in *Plays: Two*, London: Methuen

Bruno, Giordano (1964) *The Heroic Frenzies*, translated by P.E. Memmo, London

Bullock, Alan (1985) *The Humanist Tradition in the West*, New York

Burckhardt, Jacob (1958) *The Civilisation of the Renaissance in Italy*, ed. Benjamin Nelson and Charles Trinkhaus, two volumes, New York

——(1964) *Force and Freedom: Reflections on History*, ed. J.H. Nichols, Boston

Burke, Peter (1972) *Culture and Society in Renaissance Italy*, London

——(1987) *The Renaissance*, London

Carroll, Lewis (Charles Dodgson) (1965) *Alice through the Looking-glass*, in *The Annotated Alice*, ed. Martin Gardner, Harmondsworth: Penguin

Cassirer, Ernst (1944) *Essay on Man*, New Haven, CT: Yale University Press

——(ed.) (1948) *The Renaissance Philosophy of Man*, ed. P.O. Kristeller and J.H. Randall Jr, Chicago: University of Chicago Press

——ed. (1981) *Kant's Life and Thought* (1918), trans. James Haden, New Haven, CT: Yale University Press

Castiglione, Baldassare (1928) *The Book of the Courtier*, trans. Thomas Hoby (1561), London

Chomsky, Noam (1999) *The New Military Humanism: Lessons from Kosovo*, London: Pluto

Comte, Auguste (1853) *Positive Philosophy*, trans. Harriet Martineau, two volumes, London

Craven, W.G. (1981) *Giovanni Pico Della Mirandola: Symbol of his Age*, Geneva

Creeger, George S. (ed.) (1970) *George Eliot: A Collection of Critical Essays*, New Jersey

Cronin, Vincent (1955) *The Wise Man from the West*, London

Crowther, M.A. (1970) *Church Embattled: Religious Controversy in Mid-Victorian England*, Newton Abbot

Dante, *see* Alighieri, Dante

Dawkins, Richard (2006) *The God Delusion*, London: Bantam

Deane, Seamus (1988) *The French Revolution and Enlightenment in England, 1789–1832*, Cambridge, MA: Harvard University Press

Diamond, Jared (1992) *The Third Chimpanzee: The Evolution and Future of the Human Animal*, London: Harper

Dickens, A.G. (1972) *The Age of Humanism and Reformation*, London

Diderot, Denis (1992) *Political Writings*, ed. John Hope Mason and Robert Wokler, Cambridge: CUP

Eliot, George (1965) *Middlemarch*, Harmondsworth: Penguin

Eliot, T.S. (1920) *The Sacred Wood*, London: Faber & Faber

——(1951) *Selected Essays*, London: Faber & Faber

Fakhry, Majid (2001) *Averroes: Ibn Rushd*, Oxford: One World Press

Florio, John (1587) *First Frutes*, London

——(1591) *Second Frutes*, London

Forster, E.M. (1941) *Howards End* (1910), Harmondsworth: Penguin

——(1961) *A Passage to India* (1924), Harmondsworth: Penguin

——(1965) *Two Cheers for Democracy* (1951), Harmondsworth: Penguin

Foucault, Michel (1970) *The Order of Things*, London

——(1972) *The Archaeology of Knowledge*, trans. Alan Sheridan, London

——(1986) *The History of Sexuality, vol. 2: The Use of Pleasure*, Harmondsworth: Penguin

Gay, Peter (1970) *The Enlightenment: An Interpretation, vol. 1: The Rise of Modern Paganism*, London

Gelder, H.A. Enno van (1964) *The Two Reformations of the Sixteenth Century*, trans. J.F. Finlay, The Hague

Gellius, Aulus (1967) *Noctes Atticae*, trans. J.C. Rolfe, Cambridge, MA, and London: Loeb

Gibson, William (1995a, first published 1984) *Neuromancer*, London: Voyager

——(1995b) *Visions of Heaven and Hell*, London

Gobineau, Henri Arthur (1970) *Selected Political Writings*, ed. M.D. Biddiss, London

Goldmann, Lucien (1964) *The Hidden God*, London

Goodman, Lenn E. (2003) *Islamic Humanism*, Oxford: OUP

Gray, John (2002) *Straw Dogs: Thoughts on Humans and Other Animals*, London: Granta

Greenblatt, Stephen (1980) *Renaissance Self-fashioning: From More to Shakespeare*, Chicago: University of Chicago Press

Guignan, Charles (1993) *The Cambridge Companion to Heidegger*, Cambridge: CUP

Haight, Gordon S. (ed.) (1954–5) *The George Eliot Letters*, New Haven, CT: Yale University Press

——(1968) *George Eliot: A Biography*, Oxford: OUP

Haraway, Donna (2000) 'A Cyborg Manifesto', in Neil Badminton (ed.), *Post-humanism*, London: Palgrave

Hardy, Thomas (1995) *The Return of the Native* (1878), London

Hayles, M. Katherine (1999) *How We Became Posthuman: Virtual Bodies in Cybernetics, Literature and Informatics*, Chicago: University of Chicago Press

Heidegger, Martin (1971) *Poetry, Language, Thought*, trans. A. Hofstadter, New York

——(1976) 'Brief an den Humanismus', in *Gesamtausgabe*, volume 9, Frankfurt

——(1984) *Nietzsche*, volume 3, ed. David Farrell Krell, San Francisco

——(1987) *Nietzsche*, volume 4, ed. David Farrell Krell, San Francisco

Hitchens, Christopher (2007) *God Is Not Great*, New York: Warner

Hollingdale, R.J. (1973) *Nietzsche*, London

Hughes, Ted (1964) *Wodwo*, London: Faber & Faber

Hughes, Thomas (1989) *Tom Brown's Schooldays* (1857), London, ed. Andrew Sanders, Oxford

Hulme, T.E. (1924) *Speculations*, London

Hume, David (1978) *A Treatise of Human Nature* (1739–40), ed. L.A. Selby-Bigge and P.H. Hilditch, Oxford

Hutson, Lorna (1994) *The Usurer's Daughter: Male Friendship and Fictions of Women in Sixteenth-century England*, London

James, Henry (1966) *The Bostonians* (1886), Harmondsworth: Penguin

Jardine, Lisa (1974) *Francis Bacon: Discovery and the Art of Discourse*, Cambridge: CUP

——(1993) *Erasmus, Man of Letters: The Construction of Charisma in Print*, Princeton, NJ: Princeton University Press

——and Brotton, Jerry (2000) *Global Interests: Renaissance Arts between East and West*, London: Reaktion

Jeffers, Robinson (1965) *Selected Poems*, New York: Vintage

Johnson, Samuel (1906) *Lives of the Poets* (1779), London

Jonson, Ben (1975) *Complete Poems*, ed. George Parfitt, Harmondsworth: Penguin

Kant, Immanuel (1867) *Sämmtliche Werke*, ed. G. Hartenstein, Leipzig

Kraemer, Joel (1986) *Humanism in the Renaissance of Islam*, Leiden: Brill

Lacoue-Labarthe, Philippe (1990) *Heidegger, Art and Politics: The Fiction of the Political*, trans. Chris Turner, Oxford: Blackwell

Lawrence, D.H. (1981) *The Letters of D. H. Lawrence*, ed. J. T. Boulton, vol. 2, Cambridge: CUP

Leavis, F.R. (1962) *The Common Pursuit*, Harmondsworth: Penguin

Leibniz, G.W. (1697) 'Preface' to *Novissima Sinica* ('Latest News from China'), Berlin

Levi, A.W. (1969) *Humanism and Politics*, Bloomington, IN

Lloyd, Genevieve (1993) *The Man of Reason: 'Male' and 'Female' in Western Philosophy*, second edition, London: Routledge

Lukács, Georg (1969) *The Historical Novel* (1937), trans. Hannah and Stanley Mitchell, Harmondsworth: Penguin

Lukács, Georg, Benjamin, Walter and Brecht, Bertolt (1971) *Aesthetics and Politics*, London: Verso

Lyotard, Jean-François (1984) *The Postmodern Condition: A Report on Knowledge*, trans. Geoff Bennington and Brian Massumi, Manchester: Manchester University Press

——(1991) *The Inhuman: Reflections on Time*, trans. Geoff Benington and Rachel Bowlby, London

McCarthy, Cormac (2006) *The Road*, New York: Alfred A. Knopf

Machiavelli, Niccolò (1961) *The Letters of Machiavelli*, ed. Allan Gilbert, Chicago: University of Chicago Press

——(1988) *The Prince*, trans. Russell Price, ed. Quentin Skinner, Cambridge: CUP

Makdisi, George A. (1990) *The Rise of Humanism in Islam and the West*, Edinburgh: Edinburgh University Press

Mandela, Nelson (1994) Inaugural speech as President of South Africa, *Time*, 24 January 1994

Mandron, Robert (1979) *From Humanism to Science*, Brighton

Mann, Thomas (1968) *Doctor Faustus*, trans. H.T. Lowe-Porter, Harmondsworth: Penguin

——(1983) *Reflections of a Nonpolitical Man* (1918), trans. Walter D. Morris, New York

Markovic, Mihaelo (1975) *The Rise and Fall of Socialist Humanism: A History of the Praxis Group*, Nottingham: Nottingham University Press

Marlowe, Christopher (1969) *Complete Plays*, ed. J.B. Steane, Harmondsworth: Penguin

Marx, Karl (1973a) *Grundrisse: Foundations of the Critique of Political Economy*, ed. Martin Nicolaus, Harmondsworth: Penguin

——(1973b) *Surveys from Exile*, ed. David Fernbach, Harmondsworth: Penguin

——(1975) *Early Writings*, ed. Rodney Livingstone and Gregor Benton, Harmondsworth: Penguin

——and Engels, F. (1968) *Selected Works*, London

Mazower, Mark (1993) *Inside Hitler's Greece*, New Haven, CT: Yale University Press

Mill, John Stuart (1873) *Autobiography*, London

——(1962) *Utilitarianism, On Liberty, Essay on Bentham*, ed. Mary Warnock, London

——(1969) *Auguste Comte and Positivism* (1865), in *Collected Works*, volume 10, ed. F.E.L. Priestley and J.M. Robson, Toronto

Milton, John (1953) *Complete Prose Works*, vol. 1, New Haven, CT: Yale University Press

——(1971) *History of Britain*, in *Complete Prose Works*, vol. 5, Part 1, ed. French Fogle, New Haven, CT: Yale University Press

——(1990) *Complete Poems, Of Education, Areopagitica*, ed. Gordon Campbell, London

More, Thomas (1931–9) *English Works*, ed. W.E. Campbell *et al.*, London

——(1961) *Selected Letters*, ed. E.F. Rogers, New Haven, CT: Yale University Press

——(1965) *Complete Works*, volume 4, ed. Edward Surtz and J.H. Hexter, New Haven, CT: Yale University Press

——(1989) *Utopia*, trans. and ed. G.M. Logan and R.M. Adams, Cambridge: CUP

Morton, A.L. (1978) *The English Utopia*, London

Nietzsche, Friedrich (1973) *The Portable Nietzsche*, trans. and ed. Walter Kaufmann, New York

O'Malley, John W. (1993) *The First Jesuits*, Cambridge, MA: Harvard University Press

Pater, Walter (1873) *The Renaissance*, London

Petrosyan, Maria Isakovna (1972) *Humanism* (1964), trans. B. Bean and R. Daglish, Moscow: Progress Publishers

Plato (1928) *Theaetetus*, trans. H.N. Fowler, New York: Loeb

Pocock, J.G.A. (1993) 'Empire, Revolution and the End of Early Modernity', in J.G.A. Pocock (ed.), *The Varieties of British Political Thought 1500–1800*, Cambridge: CUP

Pope, Alexander (1956) *Collected Poems*, ed. Bonamy Dobree, London: Dent

Ralegh, Walter (1614) *A History of the World*, London

Rimbaud, Arthur (1962) *Poems and Letters*, ed. Oliver Bernard, Harmondsworth: Penguin

Rockmore, Tom (1995) *Heidegger and French Philosophy*, London

Ruskin, John (1865) *Sesame and Lilies*, London

Sagar, Keith (1975) *The Art of Ted Hughes*, Cambridge: CUP

Sartre, Jean-Paul (1948) *Existentialism and Humanism*, trans. P. Mairet, London

——(1961) 'Preface' to Frantz Fanon, *Les Damnés de la terre*, Paris: Maspéro (trans. as *The Wretched of the Earth*, London: Macgibbon and Key, 1965)

Schiller, F.C.S. (1907) *Studies in Humanism*, London

Schochet, Gordon J. (1993) 'Why Should History Matter? Political Theory and the History of Discourse', in J.G.A. Pocock (ed.), *The Varieties of British Political Thought 1500–1800*, Cambridge: CUP

Sidney, Philip (1965) *An Apology for Poetry*, edited by Geoffrey Shepherd, London

Singer, Peter (1990) *Animal Liberation*, New York: Random House

Skinner, Quentin, with Eckhard Kessler and Jill Kraye (eds) (1988) *The Cambridge History of Renaissance Philosophy*, Cambridge: CUP

Sloane, Thomas O. (1985) *Donne, Milton and the End of Humanist Rhetoric*, Berkeley, CA: University of California Press

Smeed, J.W. (1975) *Faust in Literature*, London

Soper, Kate (1986) *Humanism and Antihumanism*, London

——(1990) *Troubled Pleasures: Writings on Politics, Gender and Hedonism*, London: Verso

——(1995) *What Is Nature?*, London

Spenser, Edmund (1912) *Poetical Works*, ed. J.C. Smith and E. de Selincourt, London: OUP

Stedman-Jones, G. (ed.) (1977) *Western Marxism: A Critical Reader*, London

Steeves, H. Peter (ed.) (1999) *Animal Others: On Ethics, Ontology and Animal Life*, New York: SUNY Press

Steiner, George (1969) *Language and Silence*, Harmondsworth: Penguin

Swingewood, Alan (1977) *The Myth of Mass Culture*, London

Symonds, J.A. (1898) *The Renaissance in Italy*, two volumes, London

Taylor, A.L. (1952) *The White Knight*, London

Thompson, E.P. (1978) *The Poverty of Theory and Other Essays*, London

Weber, Max (1930) *The Protestant Ethic and the Spirit of Capitalism*, trans. Talcott Parsons, London

Wilde, Oscar (1954) 'The Soul of Man under Socialism' (1891), in *Selected Essays and Poems*, Harmondsworth: Penguin

Williamson, Audrey (1973) *Thomas Paine: His Life, Work and Times*, London

Yeats, W.B. (1961) *Essays and Introductions*, New York: Macmillan

Index